BBC

W9-BRN-629

VOLUME 19

LUKE

Orion N. Hutchinson, Jr.

ABINGDON PRESS
Nashville

Luke

This book is printed on recycled, acid-free paper.

Library of Congress Cataloging-in-Publication Data

Cokesbury basic Bible commentary.
  Basic Bible commentary / by Linda B. Hinton . . . [et.al.].
    p. cm.
  Originally published: Cokesbury basic Bible commentary. Nashville: Graded Press, © 1988.
  ISBN 0-687-02620-2 (pbk. : v. 1 : alk. paper)
  1. Bible—Commentaries. I. Hinton, Linda B. II. Title.
[BS491.2.C65   1994]
220.7—dc20

94-10965
CIP

ISBN 0-687-02638-5 (v. 19, Luke)
ISBN 0-687-02620-2 (v. 1, Genesis)
ISBN 0-687-02621-0 (v. 2, Exodus–Leviticus)
ISBN 0-687-02622-9 (v. 3, Numbers–Deuteronomy)
ISBN 0-687-02623-7 (v. 4, Joshua–Ruth)
ISBN 0-687-02624-5 (v. 5, 1–2 Samuel)
ISBN 0-687-02625-3 (v. 6, 1–2 Kings)
ISBN 0-687-02626-1 (v. 7, 1–2 Chronicles)
ISBN 0-687-02627-X (v. 8, Ezra–Esther)
ISBN 0-687-02628-8 (v. 9, Job)
ISBN 0-687-02629-6 (v. 10, Psalms)
ISBN 0-687-02630-X (v. 11, Proverbs–Song of Solomon)
ISBN 0-687-02631-8 (v. 12, Isaiah)
ISBN 0-687-02632-6 (v. 13, Jeremiah–Lamentations)
ISBN 0-687-02633-4 (v. 14, Ezekiel–Daniel)
ISBN 0-687-02634-2 (v. 15, Hosea–Jonah)
ISBN 0-687-02635-0 (v. 16, Micah–Malachi)
ISBN 0-687-02636-9 (v. 17, Matthew)
ISBN 0-687-02637-7 (v. 18, Mark)
ISBN 0-687-02639-3 (v. 20, John)
ISBN 0-687-02640-7 (v.21, Acts)
ISBN 0-687-02642-3 (v. 22, Romans)
ISBN 0-687-02643-1 (v. 23, 1–2 Corinthians)
ISBN 0-687-02644-X (v. 24, Galatians–Ephesians)
ISBN 0-687-02645-8 (v. 25, Philippians–2 Thessalonians)
ISBN 0-687-02646-6 (v. 26, 1 Timothy–Philemon)
ISBN 0-687-02647-4 (v. 27, Hebrews)
ISBN 0-687-02648-2 (v. 28, James–Jude)
ISBN 0-687-02649-0 (v. 29, Revelation)
ISBN 0-687-02650-4 (complete set of 29 vols.)

94 95 96 97 98 99 00 01 02 03—10 9 8 7 6 5 4 3 2 1

MANUFACTURED IN THE UNITED STATES OF AMERICA

Contents

Outline of Luke

Introduction to Luke

The Relationships Among the Gospels

Why does our Bible have four accounts of the life of Jesus? In Luke you will find much of what is in Matthew and Mark and a little of what is recorded in John. Perhaps your own experience may give you part of the reason. Do you recall a recent occasion when some important news event took place in which you had a keen interest? So significant was that event that each television and radio station was reporting what it had observed and learned about it. You found yourself turning from station to station to secure more data or the latest information. One reporter may have had information not known by another. So it is with the accounts of the life of Jesus.

Each writer brought his own background, conversations, observations, and concern to the written account. They had certain people in mind to whom they wanted to make a witness and they had certain convictions about Jesus which they wanted to convey. Placing the accounts together makes a more comprehensive picture of who Jesus was as well as what Jesus taught and did. (See the section on sources in the Introduction to Matthew for more data on these sources.)

The Writer of the Gospel

Luke was writing as a non-Jew and was probably the only non-Jewish writer of a Gospel. Through the Gospel and the Book of Acts he wanted to let the world know that Christ was for all persons—not just for Jews. For Luke was a citizen of the world.

When you pick up this Gospel, remember that you are looking at the first part of a two-part work. The Book of Acts is the second section. Both books appear to have been written by the same author and are addressed to the same unknown individual, Theophilus. At the outset of the Gospel he refers to other narratives *of the things which have been fulfilled among us* (1:1). He indicates his desire to *write an orderly account for you* (1:3).

In his introduction to Acts Luke states that in the Gospel he dealt with all that Jesus began to do and teach, *until the day when he was taken up* (Acts 1:1-2). Acts is a sequel to Luke and presents what happened after Jesus' ascension through the acts of the apostles and the activity of the Holy Spirit.

In Acts we learn that Luke was actively involved in the life of the early Christian community and was a close companion and coworker of Paul himself (See Acts 16:11-18; 20:5-21:18; 27:1-28:16). In 2 Timothy 4:11 we read *only Luke is with me.* In Philemon Paul speaks of Luke as a *fellow worker* (Philemon 24). In Romans Paul speaks of a person named *Lucius* (Romans 16:21) whom he identifies as his kinsman or fellow countryman. Some think this may be a reference to Luke. We do know from Acts that Luke journeyed with Paul to Rome on what appears to have been Paul's last journey, and that as a prisoner.

Paul also gives us the famous identification of Luke as a physician. In his letter to the Colossians he writes: "Luke the beloved physician, and Demas greet you," (Colossians 4:14). A physician had a high standing in the first century. Undoubtedly this background has some bearing upon what we find included in this Gospel. Luke describes Jesus as a person with unusual understanding of and compassion for persons. Jesus is especially concerned for those in a misunderstood minority or those whose hurts have been overlooked. As a physician, Luke may have had and understood those feelings himself. Out of his own sensitivity, he may have seen this same understanding nature and helpful outreach in Christ (but to a greater degree), and, if so, he wanted others to know it too.

The Content of Luke

The writer never identifies himself as a physician, but this designation is consistent with the concerns revealed in this Gospel. Persons appear to be more important than systems and structures. The extensive account of Jesus' travels through Samaria and his attitude toward Samaritans illustrate these concerns. The prominence Luke gives to women in his narratives are another illustration. Although Luke states his purpose to be the writing of *an orderly account* of what had been heard from eyewitnesses, he seems to have been even more interested in writing *an orderly account* of the nature and compassion of Jesus.

Luke begins at the very beginning. He tells us more about the events surrounding the birth of Jesus than any of the other Gospels. These impressive events are to underline the spiritual importance of the personhood of Jesus. Luke introduces us to John the Baptist and includes the account of his baptizing Jesus with a description which again underlines the spiritual significance of Jesus. To strengthen his case, Luke provides a genealogy that traces the ancestry of Jesus back to David, Abraham, Noah, and Adam—a line of spiritual heroes from the days of Creation.

The narration of the ministry of Jesus begins in his home town, Nazareth, and the synagogue there. It moves out from there to surrounding areas until ultimately it ends in Jerusalem. Basically Luke describes three phases of ministry and witness: in the area of Galilee (4:1-9:50), en route to Jerusalem (9:51-19:44), and in or near

Jerusalem (19:45-21:38). The larger portion of the narrative relates to the ministry enroute to Jerusalem. Especially in this portion, we see Jesus encountering many different types of persons, responding to each one in ways appropriate to his or her needs.

This Gospel has other distinctive characteristics. For one thing, the Greek language in which it was written gives evidence of being the best-educated use of Greek in the New Testament, which could be an outgrowth of Luke's mind and training as a physician. Another language characteristic is that Luke records most of the sayings of Jesus as apothegms, or short, pithy statements.

An important characteristic of this Gospel is the attention given to the Holy Spirit. This is an important characteristic of both the Gospel and Acts. There are seventeen references to the Spirit in the Gospel (compared with twelve in Matthew, six in Mark), and fifty-seven references in Acts. The presence and work of the Holy Spirit are prominent especially in the beginning of both books. In Luke the Spirit is related to the stories of Zechariah; Gabriel; and Mary, Elizabeth, and Simeon. Acts begins with the story of Pentecost. From Luke's perspective Jesus and the church lived and ministered through the enablement of the Holy Spirit. Thus it is not surprising to discover that the prayer and devotional experiences of Jesus occupy an important place in Luke.

Among the materials Luke includes that are not in the other Gospels are five miracle events, six parables, including that of the Good Samaritan, and special events such as the story of Zacchaeus, the trial before Herod, the thief on the cross, and the walk to Emmaus.

No one knows the exact date of the writing of this Gospel. The earliest projected date is about A.D. 75, but the prevalent opinion of Bible scholars places its writing later, in the 80s or 90s. It would have been about the same time as Matthew, and after Mark, since it includes much of Mark in its contents.

Introduction to This Chapter

In a sense this first chapter is an introduction to the entire book. Here you will find stated the person to whom the book is addressed, the reason for its being written, and the background for the birth of Jesus. Some themes are sounded that will reappear in various forms later in the narrative. Some sensitivities are demonstrated that become the mark of Luke's style. The chapter tells us of the angelic announcements to Zechariah and Elizabeth of the impending birth of their son, John the Baptist, and to Mary of her role to be the earthly mother of the messiah.

The chapter may be outlined as follows:
  I. The Author's Purpose (1:1-4)
  II. The Announcement to Zechariah (1:5-25)
  III. The Announcement to Mary (1:26-56)
  IV. The Birth of John the Baptist (1:57-80)
The narrative begins with a setting in the Temple in Jerusalem, and then moves to Nazareth, the home of Mary and Joseph.

The Author's Purpose (1:1-4)

Theophilus is identified as the one to whom this book is addressed. The book of Acts in the New Testament is also addressed to him. Thus the two books were intended to be companion-pieces, one relating the story of Jesus obtained from "eyewitnesses," and the other reporting the spread of the gospel through the enablement of the Holy Spirit after Jesus *was taken up* (Acts 1:2). In Acts Luke speaks of the Gospel as *the first book* in which he dealt with all that Jesus began to do and teach (Acts 1:1). In the Gospel itself Luke implies that he has observed the accounts of *many* eyewitnesses. Benefitting from these, he now wishes to write, as an observer, *an orderly account.*

Theophilus is not identified except by the title *most excellent,* a title usually used for high Roman officials. In Acts 23:26; 24:2; and 26:25 it is used for the Roman procurator of Judea. Thus this material most probably was prepared primarily for a non-Jewish personage or audience. The name means friend of God. So he may be a Gentile convert or a representative of non-Jewish persons who were open to and interested in the truth about Christ.

The Announcement to Zechariah (1:5-25)

There was a family dynasty ruling the Jewish area of Judea under Roman authority from 37 B.C. to A.D. 70 known as the Herods. The Herod named in verse 5 was known as Herod the Great. Judea was the region in southern Palestine west of the northern part of the Dead Sea.

Zechariah was one of the priests in the Temple at Jerusalem. The priesthood was divided into twenty-four groups who attended to the priestly duties in shifts. Each group was named after one of the earliest priests, of whom Abijah was one.

In the Jewish religious tradition righteousness was seen as faithful obedience to the Law of Moses and the Ten Commandments. This is illustrated in verse 6 where both Zechariah and Elizabeth are described as *righteous (NRSV) or upright* (NIV) because they walked in all the *commandments and regulations* of the Lord blameless (see also Philippians 3:6b). It is interesting to note that the

12   LUKE

name of the wife of Aaron, the first person in the line of priests, was also a form of Elizabeth (Exodus 6:23). Although she also is thought to have been of priestly descent, women could not serve as priests at this time in history.

In the Temple from the beginning (see Exodus 30:1) there was an altar of incense in the Holy Place, a section of the Temple. At least twice daily incense was burned, in the morning when the lamps were extinguished and in the evening when the lamps were lighted. The fragrance of incense spreading throughout the Temple was representative of God's presence and Spirit filling the Holy Place. Zechariah was carrying out this traditional act of worship as a priest when the angelic visitation took place (verse 9).

Zechariah is described as *terrified* (NRSV) with the *angelic encounter (verse 12). This word can also be translated as startled* (NIV).

For a Jewish couple to have no children was not only a great personal disappointment, but at times was seen as a form of spiritual failure. The first guideline given in the scriptural tradition was to *be fruitful and multiply* (Genesis 1:28). At the time of marriage there was a prayer that the new wife might be "as a fruitful vine." Children were seen as a sign of divine blessing. It was through children, especially a son, that the family line was preserved and fulfilled. Thus, not to have children was frequently seen as a curse. So Elizabeth and Zechariah, having aged beyond the usual child-bearing years, must have lived with nagging disappointment and fear of spiritual failure and perplexity in her barrenness (verse 7). The news that they were to become parents as part of the divine plan would not only be stunning news—this is why he asks, How shall I know this? (verse 18)—but thrilling news of spiritual fulfillment (verse 14). The name *John* means *God has been gracious.*

To drink *no wine nor other fermented drink* (NIV) or

strong drink (NRSV) (verse 15) meant living a self-disciplined life in the spirit and style of the Nazirites (see Numbers 6), who dedicated themselves to God and took upon themselves this obligation.

In verse 17 the pronoun *him* (NRSV) refers to God or *The Lord* (NIV). The description of John's calling to go *before* God in *the spirit and power of Elijah* refers back to an Old Testament tradition about the messiah. In Malachi 4:5 appears the declaration that the prophet Elijah will be sent *before the great and terrible* (NRSV) or *dreadful* (NIV) *Day of the Lord comes.* A prophet was one who spoke for God. For Elijah, a pioneer in the line of prophets, to return would symbolically say that God is speaking again in a special way.

The word *angel* literally means *messenger.* Angels were seen as a set of beings who resided close to the throne or dwelling-place of God and were sent on missions to convey divine messages. There was even thought to be a structure or heirarchy of angels, with Gabriel (verse 19) being a superior angel, or archangel. The name *Gabriel* means *hero of God* or *God has shown a mighty selfhood.* He is introduced in the Bible in Daniel 8:16-17 as one who explained a vision to Daniel. Additional episodes about Gabriel are found in two books, 1 and 2 Enoch, which were written between the Old and New Testaments. So the Jewish readers of this Gospel would have known who Gabriel was.

For Zechariah not to be able to speak (verse 20) would be an experience similar to Daniel, who was made speechless after a divine visitation (see Daniel 10:15). Both Daniel and Zechariah later were given the restoration of speech (verses 64-79). So we see certain parallels in this story between events recorded in Daniel and the experiences of Zechariah, both highly figurative and symbolic accounts.

The Announcement to Mary (1:26-56)
The *sixth month* (verse 26) probably refers back to the months of Elizabeth's pregnancy. In the sixth month of

Elizabeth's pregnancy Mary received the angel's visit. Regarding angels, and Gabriel in particular, see the previous comments on verse 19.

Pledged (NIV) or *engaged* (NRSV) means a formalized commitment to marry, almost as binding in Jewish tradition as marriage itself, expressed before witnesses. The Greek word for *virgin* (verse 27), translated *girl* in the *New English Bible*, meant a young woman of marriageable age who had not yet married, and thus presumably had not had sexual intercourse.

The Jewish messianic tradition identified the line of David as the line of descent through which the messiah would come. Thus Joseph's identification as being of the house of David is important for that reason. In Luke 3:23-38 we find the genealogy of Jesus through the ancestry of Joseph as listed there in detail. Joseph is only mentioned in the Gospels in connection with the birth narratives. He is presumed to have been a carpenter because of the comment in the Gospel of Mark about Jesus being a carpenter (Mark 6:3).

The greeting, *Greetings, you who are highly favored* (NIV) or *Greeting, O favored one* (NRSV) (verse 28) has found its way into our Christian tradition of worship and music in the form of *Ave Maria*, which is a rendering of this verse.

The name *Jesus* (verse 31) is a Greek rendering of the name *Joshua*, familiar from the Old Testament tradition. It means *the Lord is salvation*.

Verses 32-33 are indented in the NRSV. Wherever the text is printed in this form, it indicates quotations and/or poetry. Of course, we are reading an English translation of Hebrew words. In Hebrew, poetry is distinguished by accent rhythms and repeition of thoughts in couplets rather than rhyming words. These verses are not direct quotes of Old Testament words but they do include many phrases found in Old Testament passages, which would be very familiar to Jewish readers, and many of which had become associated with the messiah to come. You

can find some of these images in 2 Samuel 7:13-16;
Psalms 2:7 and 89:26-27; and Isaiah 9:6-7.

The house of Jacob (verse 33) is a more comprehensive
phrase for the line of promise, and all the descendants of
that line scattered worldwide, which goes back to
Abraham and God's covenant with him (see Genesis 17:2;
27:29).

Mary and Elizabeth are thought to have been cousins;
thus the word *relative* is used (verse 36).

Judah (verse 39) is the same as Judea (see comments on
verse 5).

The lines beginning *Blessed are you among women . . .*
are the second part of the frequently used prayer in the
Roman Catholic tradition beginning *Hail, Mary (Ave,
Maria;* see comment on verse 28).

The verses beginning with 46 through verse 55
compose that Scripture portion known as the Magnificat,
which is a Latin word for *magnify* (NRSV) or *glorifies*
(NIV) found in the first line. It might be considered the
first Christian hymn. This beautiful and memorable
passage has some parallel in the Song of Hannah
(1 Samuel 2:1-10) as she rejoiced over the birth of her
long-desired child, Samuel.

The Birth of John the Baptist (1:57-80)

Circumcision (verse 59) was the rite of initiation for a
male Jew into the covenant relationship with God. It
involved the cutting off of the foreskin covering the male
sexual organ. The custom originated at the time of God's
covenant with Abraham (see Genesis 17:9-14), and
symbolized the offering of one's present powers and
relationships and children to come to a covenant with
God to be obedient to the law and commandments and
walk with God all one's days.

Regarding the restoration of speech to Zechariah
(verse 64), see the earlier commentary on verse 20.

The psalm or song of Zechariah (verses 68-79) is a

testimony of gratitude, not just over the birth of John, but over the realization that the long-promised messiah is indeed coming, and coming soon. Verses 68-75 celebrate the messiah's coming and verses 76-79 the strategic role of John the Baptist in relation to the messiah. There John is identified as being in the line of prophets. The entire psalm is made up of phrases and figures of speech used numerous times in the Old Testament. It underlines for the Jewish reader that these nativity events are fulfillments of the Old Testament promises made as far back as Abraham (verse 73). The keynote given in verse 69 is that a *horn of salvation* (NIV) or *mighty savior* (NRSV) has been *raised up* by God. This figure used in Old Testament imagery signifies power or strength.

Periods of preparation and spiritual self-examination were essential to fulfilling God's expectation as servants called to special tasks. Thus John went to *the wilderness* for such (verse 80). Later Jesus would do the same (4:1).

§ § § § § § §

The Message of Luke 1

At the risk of being overly simple, there are two striking discoveries the reader of this Gospel can receive while reading the story of the announcements to Elizabeth and Zechariah and Mary and Joseph along with the sudden change of events in their lives. One discovery is that you can never count God out. The Lord is always doing the unexpected to and through unexpecting, but hopeful, people, open to divine purposes and power. Our God is the God who acts with amazing but fulfilling surprises. The second discovery is that the Almighty never counts us out. God still comes to us, often when we least expect it, with new possibilities for life and new purposes to life.

But, as it is written, "What no eye has seen, nor ear heard, nor the heart of man or mind conceived, what God has prepared for those who love him," God has revealed to us through the Spirit (1 Corinthians 2:9-10). And the Spirit, through Luke's witness, has revealed these things through the events in this chapter.

§ § § § § § §

LUKE 2

Introduction to This Chapter

This chapter brings us the familiar nativity story and also the only stories in the Gospels about the childhood of Jesus. It is a beautiful narrative intended to affirm through its unusual events that God was moving into the midst of humanity in an unusual way. Little can be said to add in any way to the loveliness of the contents, but some explanations may add to our understanding of those contents, which are as follows:

I. The Birth of Jesus (2:1-21)
II. Presentation and Affirmation (2:22-38)
III. The Childhood of Jesus (2:39-52)

The Birth of Jesus (2:1-21)

Caesar Augustus was the Roman emperor from 26 B.C. to A.D. 14. *Caesar* was the title of the ruler and *Augustus* was the name given him by the Roman Senate after he assumed the office. Previously his name was Gaius Octavius, and he was a nephew of Julius Caesar. Quirinius—a correction of Cyrenius as stated in the King James Version—was appointed governor in A.D. 6 and took a census, or registration of the population, about A.D. 8. Here some confusion exists because Herod the Great, identified by Luke as ruler at this time (1:5), died before Quirinius assumed office. Therefore, there is an historical discrepancy that makes it difficult to identify the exact year of Jesus' birth.

The method of registration of the population as stated

here was for each to return to his *own town* (verse 3) or homeplace of the family group. Bethlehem, meaning *house of bread*, was the ancestral home of the line of David (see 1 Samuel 17:15). Joseph was a descendant of David (3:23, 31), and thus would go to Bethlehem with any family members he had to register. They traveled from Nazareth, a village in Galilee fifteen miles southwest of the Sea of Galilee, where Mary and Joseph had been living (1:26).

Verse 7 reports specifically on the birth of Jesus. These transients found no room at the local inn, since the town would have been thronged with visitors for the required registration. They apparently found shelter in a bedding place for farm animals. This could well have been a cave, for such are still used today for animal shelters or for shelter by nomadic families in the Middle East. Here they would find privacy, some comfort on the grasses or straw left over from feeding, and some protection from storm or sun. The wrapping of a baby in bands of cloth, completely encircling the body, was a cultural custom.

The baby is referred to as the *firstborn*, thus implying that other children were born later to Mary. Mark names four such brothers and suggests that there were at least two sisters (Mark 6:3).

For shepherds to be with their sheep at night was not unusual in Palestine. Shepherds moved with their flocks from place to place seeking enough plant growth for the sheep to feed upon in the midst of dry, arid countryside. These nomadic shepherds might carry tents with them to use for longer stays in one area. However, often they simply camped out in the open. Some of the spiritual insights of the Old Testament were likely received in such a setting (see, for example, Psalms 19 and 23).

Once again an angel appears as a messenger (verse 9). Awed by this unexpected glorious confrontation, the shepherds were frightened, just as were Zechariah (1:12) and Mary (1:29). In all three incidents, the angel first sought to relieve that sense of fear. One need not be afraid of a message from God. Here is where the Greek word *gospel* occurs in the text. It means *good news* (verse 10). Interestingly, the good news was that a homeless couple had brought forth a child, whose coming was for each and every wanderer upon the face of the earth, to whom it was first announced. In this child each could find a personal (to you is born) savior and the Messiah (NRSV; *Christ,* NIV), in whom God would be present (*the Lord*).

The anthem of the *heavenly host* (verse 14) is commonly known by the Latin wording *gloria in excelsis,* which states the first line. It affirms that God merits the highest glory for this divine entrance in and among humanity in Jesus. To express *glory* is to offer the highest praise.

As the shepherds went to Bethlehem (*city of David*), the two marks by which they were to identify the Christ child were the cloth wrappings and the manger location (verses 12, 16).

The Jewish law provided that every male child was to be circumcised (see commentary on 1:59) on the eighth day after birth (Leviticus 12:3). This covenant rite was exercised upon Jesus.

Presentation and Affirmation 2:22-38)

Mary and Joseph appear to have had a deep respect for the traditions of Scripture and the Jewish community of which they were a part. This is illustrated in the events reported here.

According to Jewish law, for forty days after a son's birth the mother was to remain in isolation from ceremonies and social events, and after a daughter's birth for eighty days (see Leviticus 12). These were called the days of purification, and allowed for the restoration of the body. When the purification period ended, a sin-offering was to be made to the Lord. Thus verse 22 speaks of the time of purification *according to the law of Moses* when the parents took the baby to Jerusalem.

Verse 23 contains a quotation taken from Exodus 13:1-2, calling for the dedication of every male child to God.

The sacrifice mentioned in verse 24 is a pair of turtledoves or *two young pigeons.* Actually, the law called for the offering of a yearling ram as a sacrifice for purification. However, the law provided that if the new mother could not afford a ram, she could bring two turtledoves or young pigeons, one for a whole offering and one for a sin offering. In the case of Mary and Joseph, they brought the offerings of poorer people, indicating that they were of the peasant population.

Simeon is mentioned only in this passage (verse 25), and nothing is really known about him. His looking for the *consolation of Israel* meant that he was looking for God's promised messiah. He was in the Temple when Jesus was brought to be offered to the Lord as the law required (do for him according to the custom of the law, verse 27). There is a possibility that Simeon was the priest on duty in the Temple when the presentation of Jesus was to take place. Simeon did take Jesus *in his arms* (verse 28) as a priest might do and also blessed the parents (verse 34).

Verses 29-32 consist of a prayer of commitment or psalm known to many by the Latin title *Nunc Dimittis*. This is a Latin rendering of a part of the first line, *Now dismiss your servant*. The basic idea in the prayer is the confession that Simeon was willing to die, because his long-held hope to see God's promised one had been fulfilled in the coming of this child whom the Spirit had identified to Simeon as the Messiah. In the psalm you will find echoes of several Old Testament figures of speech (see Isaiah 42:6; 49:6; 52:10).

Verse 32 has a special significance because it announces that Jesus has been given for both Gentiles and Jews. Luke will have that conviction in mind as he presents material in this Gospel. Christ is for all persons.

The words to Mary (verses 34-35) sound the first sinister note concerning the fate of Jesus. It is a soft note now which will be louder as time passes.

Anna is another person mentioned only in Luke (verses 36-38). Although women were not priests, they did serve in the line of prophets. Her name means *grace*. She was married only seven years, and was now eighty-four years old. Those who were looking for *the redemption of Israel* were, like Simeon, those looking and praying for the messiah to come.

The Childhood of Jesus (2:39-52)

In verse 39 Nazareth is again identified as the residence of the family. No mention is made in Luke of the flight to Egypt to escape Herod's slaughter (see Matthew 2:13-23).

The Feast of the Passover celebrated the angel of death passing over the home of Hebrew slaves during the plagues in Egypt (Exodus 12). All faithful Jews sought to make a pilgrimage to the Temple in Jerusalem during their lifetime, and annually if possible. The preferred occasion for this pilgrimage was during the feast of the Passover. Mary and Joseph made this pilgrimage annually, indicating their spiritual devotion to the Jewish tradition. The observance lasted seven days (verse 43).

After three days (verse 46) probably includes a day of journeying home and a day of returning. Large groups of all ages would travel together in caravans, so it is not surprising that Jesus was not missed immediately.

The translation in verse 49, *be in my Father's house,* is a more accurate translation than the King James Version rendering of this question, *be about my Father's business.*

Twice in this chapter Mary is described as keeping all these things *in her heart* (verses 19, 51). This suggests a reflective person who did not completely understand what was taking place around her but kept pondering it until time would unveil the full meaning. Meanwhile, Jesus grew toward maturity in mind, body, and spirit (verses 40, 52).

§ § § § § § §

The Message of Luke 2

If there is any central theme to the varied stories in this chapter beyond their common focus on the childhood of Jesus, it is the theme of expectations fulfilled. However, the expectations were not always fulfilled in expected ways.

The shepherds were surprised and surprising as the audience for the regal announcement of the birth of the Messiah. A baby born to a peasant family was hardly the expected way for Christ to arrive. Bethlehem, although the seat of the line of David through which the messiah was to come, was certainly not ready. Yet God acted as predicted and came as promised.

The heavenly host sang. Simeon and Anna rejoiced. Mary and Joseph assumed their spiritual responsibility as parents in a diligent and faithful manner. They became stewards of the spiritual potential of the lad entrusted to their nurture (as we all should do for those entrusted to our parenting). Not fully knowing what the future might hold for Jesus, they recognized him to be the child of expectation and God's presence and responded accordingly.

Yet in the midst of rejoicing that God has come in Jesus for all humanity, forever testifying that God never abandons us, we are reminded that God often acts differently from our predictions. It may just be that God in wisdom and love sends us not quite what we want but what we actually need, even a new way of understanding where divine values are in contrast to our human wants.

§ § § § § § §

Introduction to These Chapters

The narrative in this section focuses on three primary
events: the baptism of Jesus by John the Baptist, the
temptation of Jesus in the wilderness, and the
presentation by Jesus in his home synagogue. All of these
events were important as preparation for the ministry of
Jesus and provide an insight into Jesus' own concepts of
the nature and purpose of his life. Additionally, a listing
of the ancestry of Jesus is provided by Luke to convey
not only his background but his spiritual credentials.

The material is organized as follows:
  I. John Prepares the Way (3:1-20)
 II. The Baptism of Jesus (3:21-22)
III. Ancestral Heritage of Jesus (3:23-38)
 IV. Preparatory Temptations (4:1-13)

John Prepares the Way (3:1-20)

The *fifteenth year of the reign of Emperor Tiberius* (NSRV)
or *Tiberius Caesar* (NIV) (verse 1) would have been
A.D. 28–29. Tiberius Caesar was the stepson, and later
son-in-law, of Augustus Caesar (2:1). Most of the names
listed in verses 1-2 are included not simply to give the
historical framework but also because of important roles
they will play in the later events of Jesus' life.

John was last mentioned as being in the wilderness
until *he appeared publicly to Israel* (1:80). Verse 2 picks up

John's story at this same point. He received the *word of God* there, which helps to identify John as in the prophetic line (1:76). Prophets received their calling, not by inheritance as did priests, but by the word being imparted to them by God, which they then proclaimed (see Amos 3:8). Prophets spoke for God.

The setting is the Jordan River valley (verse 3). The Jordan ran from the Sea of Galilee in the north to empty into the Dead Sea in the south. This setting is twenty-five miles east of Jerusalem.

John called for *a baptism of repentance* (verse 3). The use of water in purification rites was not new with John. It was even prescribed in Jewish law under certain circumstances (see Exodus 29:4; 30:20; Leviticus 15:13; 16:26, 28; 17:15; Numbers 19:8). However, these rites usually had to do with cleansing from an uncleanness of the body due to contact with a ceremonially unclean person. John's call was for a purification of the inside of one's being—the self—from sin. This was to be both a turning away from the past (*repentance*) and a preparation (*prepare*) for the future when God comes near in Christ.

The quotation from Isaiah 40:3-5 (verses 4-6) emphasizes the act of preparation. The original setting for this passage was the period of Jewish exile. The children of Israel had been taken to Babylonia and were separated from their homeland and the spiritual symbols there of God's presence in their midst. The prophecy confirmed that God would act and remove all the barriers that they thought separated them from home and God. John affirmed that this was also happening in the coming of the Messiah when again *all flesh shall see the salvation of God* (NRSV).

The concept of being God's chosen people since the covenant with Abraham (verse 8) had left some Jews with the false conclusion that their spiritual well-being was secure and permanent. John strongly attacked this spiritual complacency (verses 7-9). One's past spiritual heritage is no guarantee of one's present spiritual vitality.

Verses 10-14 describe the hearers' response and John's counsel. Note that John called for two types of response. One was the repentance that issued forth in baptism (verse 3). The second was a repentance that issued forth in a changed lifestyle. The essence of that change was to be a new set of priorities and a sensitivity and sharing one toward another. It was living for another's welfare and not for one's own gain. An act of cleansing alone was not sufficient without acts of caring. Tax collectors, known for their corruption and self-gain, and soldiers, known for their self-assured dominance of others, responded to John's preaching, indicating his powerful influence (verses 12-14). They also were called to a change of priorities and caring.

So powerful was John's witness and influence that his hearers began to feel he might be the promised Messiah (verse 15). John pointed to another to come who would bring more than purifying water to persons, but God's Spirit and the Spirit's fire of cleansing and enablement (verses 16-18).

Herod had married Herodias, who had first been the wife of his half-brother Philip (verse 1). John had condemned this act (verse 19-20), resulting in John's imprisonment and ultimately his death. For more details on these circumstances see Matthew 14:1-12.

The Baptism of Jesus (3:21-22)

Luke's account of the baptism of Jesus is very brief. The physical perspective here is based upon the concept that God dwelt in an area above a dome over the earth, which was the sky. The heavens being *opened* suggests God being a witness and pouring the Spirit down from heaven upon Jesus. God gave divine sufficiency to Jesus.

The *dove* had long been a special symbol. It was a symbol of peace dating back to the story of the dove bringing to Noah an olive-leaf, thus informing him that storm and destruction had ended (Genesis 8:11). The dove was also used at times to represent Israel (*Jonah* means *dove,* and in his story he represents all of Israel). Because the dove brought peace and hope, it became a symbol of God's Spirit drawing close.

The quotation in verse 22 is from Psalm 2:7. It confirmed that God's Son had come; the Messiah was here.

For an expansion of the baptismal story, see Matthew 3:13-17.

Ancestral Heritage of Jesus (3:23-38)

Previous references have been made to this genealogy and its significance. (See the commentary on 1:27.)

Verse 22 identifies the divine ancestry of Jesus as Son of God. Beginning with verse 23 the human ancestry of Jesus is traced. Here the important factor was to identify Jesus as in the line of spiritual promise, beginning with Abraham (verse 34) and reconfirmed with David (verse 31). Out of this line the messiah was to come, Luke goes even further than does Matthew (Matthew 1:1-17) in his opening genealogy. Matthew traces ancestry back to Abraham; Luke goes all the way back to Adam (verse 38). Of Adam he uses the phrase *son of God,* an affirmation just made of Jesus in verse 22. This may be to suggest that these two, and these two only, have the unique characteristic of being directly created by God's initiatives.

Preparatory Temptations (4:1-13)

The area around the Jordan Valley is a dry, arid, rocky wilderness, especially in the area around the Dead Sea, and between the Jordan Valley and Jerusalem. Jesus moved from spiritual exhilaration to spiritual desolation, as do many of us who move from spiritual "highs"to personal lows, sometimes back to back.

The *forty days* (verse 2) have no special spiritual significance except for being the time frame of some important events in Jewish history, such as the Flood (Genesis 7:4), Moses upon the mountain (Exodus 24:18),

Elijah's journey (1 Kings 19:8), and Jonah's prediction of Nineveh's overthrow (Jonah 3:4).

The three temptations follow a certain format: a visual experience that becomes symbolic, from it the suggestions of a possibility unfaithful to God's purposes, and then confrontation by Scripture.

This wilderness was a rocky area. Having fasted for forty days (verse 2). Jesus would have been very hungry. His hunger could have led him to imagine food. The round rocks could resemble loaves of bread in one's imagination (verse 3). Jesus would have had the divine power to create, thus ending his personal sacrifice chosen for spiritual ends. To this Jesus responded by quoting Deuteronomy 8:3 (verse 4).

This wilderness was also a hilly, even mountainous area. From the heights one could see vast distances in all directions, including not only Israel but neighboring countries. Perhaps one could feel as though one saw *in an instant all the kingdoms of the world* (verse 5). The devil claimed to be in possession of them (verse 6), and offered them to Jesus in exchange for his worship. To this Jesus quoted Deuteronomy 6:13 (verse 8).

From the heights of this wilderness area one could see in the distance the outline of Jerusalem on Mount Zion. This distant view may have brought to Jesus' mind the sacred Temple at the top of Mount Zion. The temptation was to take a short-cut to spiritual acclaim, rather than the long hard way of human involvement, rejection, and a cross. This time the temptor used Jesus' own method to persuade him by quoting Scripture to him, Psalm 91:11-12 (verses 10-11). Again Jesus responded with a scriptural quotation, Deuteronomy 6:16 (verse 12).

In the three temptations we have a summary of the basic temptations confronting all humanity: sense, power or possessions, and pride (see 1 John 2:16).

The temptor was not permanently rebuffed, but departed to return at *an opportune time* (verse 13).

§ § § § § § §

The Message of Luke 3:1-4:13

The rugged demands of discipleship appear in this passage. For John the Baptist, faithfulness to proclaim the message given him by God led him to a wilderness pulpit. His message would hardly have been cordially received in the community synagogue. He had to pay the price of isolation born out of conviction. This was not unusual for a prophet.

Yet the demands became even more rugged. His faithfulness led to a confrontation and condemnation with royal disregard for moral principle. This would result in his imprisonment and finally his death.

Jesus came to enter into his ministry through the door of baptism. It was an exalted and exalting moment. God was near and the Spirit was received. Jesus had the sanction of divine blessing and royal heritage. Yet from this exaltation he moved immediately into temptation. In the temptation he would have to reject physical comfort, worldly dominance, and self-serving demonstrations of power, to which his credentials would have entitled him.

The invitation to discipleship is freely offered. But the demands of faithfulness can be strenuous.

§ § § § § § §

PART FOUR Luke 4:14–5:16

Introduction to These Verses

The Spirit of the Lord is upon me because he has anointed me . . . (4:18). These words of Isaiah read by Jesus in his home synagogue can serve also as a theme for the events in this section. Having moved through the initiatory and preparatory events of baptism and temptation, Jesus emerged to begin his ministry as Son of God and Christ or Messiah. He did so by returning to his home area, Galilee (not the area of his birth in Judea). There he publicly affirmed his calling or mission and began to undertake it. His being *anointed* is given support by what he was able to do and the way people began to respond to him, moving from scepticism to acclaim and allegience toward him in this opening phase of ministry. This section may be outlined as follows:

I. At Jesus' Home Synagogue (4:14-30)
II. Ministry of Healing (4:31-41)
III. General Ministry in the Area (4:42-44)
IV. Beginnings of Enlistment (5:1-11)
V. Ministry and Meditation (5:12-16)

At Jesus' Home Synagogue (4:14-30)

Regarding Jesus' return in *the power of the Spirit,* note also previous references to the Holy Spirit in 4:1. Jesus was *led by the Spirit* into the wilderness, and having successfully overcome temptation, returned now in *the power of the Spirit.* Obviously, power had come through struggle.

31

The initial reaction to Jesus was positive. He was first seen as a teacher (verse 15) or rabbi and invited to fill this role in synagogues. *Being praised* means, as the New English Bible translates it, everyone *sang his praises*.

Back to Nazareth in Galilee he came (verses 14, 16). There his story had begun with the angel's visit to Mary (1:26) and from there the expectant parents had traveled to Bethlehem (2:4).

Jesus was giving evidence of a loyalty to the Jewish tradition and its expectations by establishing a *custom* (verse 16) of worshiping in the synagogue. In Jewish worship there was prescribed a reading from the Law and one selected from the Prophets. These were in Hebrew with translation into Aramaic, the language of the people. Usually the Law would be read by a priest, if present. Yet the elders could, and did, call upon a visiting worshiper to offer one of the readings, usually from the Prophets, as an expression of hospitality or tribute. Thus there was given to Jesus *the scroll of the prophet Isaiah.* This would have been a rolled-up scroll which he would open to the passage of his choosing.

Jesus chose Isaiah 61:1-2. This was one of the well-known passages of hope in the midst of descriptions of the messianic age made to those returning from the exile in Babylonia to their homelands of spiritual origin. It spoke of the calling of God to Israel in their new day. Now Jesus adapted it to describe his own calling as Christ, clearly affirming that *today this scripture is fulfilled in your hearing* (verse 21).

While some there *spoke well of him* (verse 22), some were skeptical. The proverb, *Physician, heal yourself* (verse 23, NIV) and the following statement were calls for Jesus to prove the claim he had made in the synagogue. The specific reference to *Capernaum* is puzzling because no prior event in Capernaum is reported by Luke. Either there was an unreported event, or this synagogue visit is out of correct order of events and happened later, as Mark suggests (Mark 6:1-4).

Verse 24 contains an often-quoted New Testament statement.

The Elijah story (verses 25-26) is found in 1 Kings 17:1-24. The Elisha story (verse 27) is found in 2 Kings 5:1-19. While it is not clearly stated in the Elijah story, apparently in both episodes the prophets reached out in ministry to non-Jewish persons. By recalling these stories to his Jewish audience, Jesus implied that even if *in his own country* he was not received, he would be reaching out in ministry and message beyond his own people. Non-Jews as well as Jews would receive his witness.

This inclusiveness can explain the anger (verse 28) of those in the synagogue who almost lynched Jesus (verse 29). They saw the messiah as the fulfillment and redemption of the Jews only. By *passing through the midst of them* (verse 30, NRSV), Jesus demonstrated his mastery and God's providential deliverance.

Ministry of Healing (4:31-41)

Nazareth was in hilly country (verse 29); Capernaum was in the valley on the northwest coast of the Sea of Galilee. Thus Jesus went *down to Capernaum* (verse 31), 686 feet below sea level. The name meant *village of Nahum*, probably in reference to the Old Testament prophet, Nahum.

Note again Jesus *teaching* (verse 32) as an itinerant rabbi. It was in the synagogue where an encounter took place.

This man who *had the spirit of an unclean demon* (verse 33, NRSV; NIV = *a demon, an evil spirit*) was a victim of mental illness. When behavior patterns became strange or abnormal, the early presumption was that such a person was no longer in control of self but had fallen under the adverse influence of some other force or being. Because the behavior was disturbing or destructive, the controlling force or power was seen as evil or demonic. Such concepts preceded awareness of the nature and forms of mental illness that would come much later in history.

The questions asked in verse 34 have several

implications. By asked *What have you to do with us?* a recognition is made of a pronounced difference between the nature of Jesus and the nature of evil. By asking *Have you come to destroy us?* the potential power of Jesus over evil is recognized. In the statement identifying Jesus as *the Holy One of God* there is affirmed that even evil forces perceive who Jesus really is.

When the man was thrown down (verse 35), he had fainted or collapsed from a psychotic break or emotional exhaustion. After this therapeutic episode, Luke reaffirms the mastery of Jesus over another area of life (verse 36).

Simon (verse 38) is abruptly introduced with no prior reference. It is only through the other Gospels that we would know at this point who Simon was. Luke may have accidentally omitted an earlier reference to Simon such as is found in Mark 1:16-18, or may have presumed that his readers would already know Simon's identity because of his prominence. This healing of a fever is intended to portray Jesus' mastery over physical illness.

Verses 40-41 summarize and reaffirm these skillful masteries of Jesus over illness of mind or spirit and body as they were even more widely demonstrated. The verbal exchange between Jesus and the demonic spirits in which Jesus would not let them speak *because they knew that he was the Christ* (NIV; NRSV = *Messiah*) is taken from Mark 3:11-12. Perhaps it was because the professions of his being the Christ would be seen only as expressions arising out of and as a part of the person's illness.

General Ministry in the Area (4:42-44)

After immense public exposure and ministry, Jesus revealed what would be a recurring pattern—to withdraw for a while alone. Yet his privacy would become more difficult to retain because of widening acclaim and popularity. The possessiveness of the people was a tribute to how Jesus met them at their points of need.

Good news (verse 43) is again used to describe the proclamation he wished to make (see again verse 18). Now Jesus added the theme of the *kingdom of God* as a primary theme as he committed himself to a wider witness. As an itinerant teacher, he traveled south to neighboring Judea (see 1:39; 2:4).

Beginnings of Enlistment (5:1-11)

The Lake of Gennesaret (verse 1), although occasionally used interchangeably for the Sea of Galilee, is actually that portion of the Sea next to a valley on the northwest shore called Gennesaret.

The prevalence of fishing in the Sea of Galilee is well known even to the casual reader of the Gospels. Since the Sea of Galilee was not far from Nazareth, the place where Jesus was raised, he probably visited there often and knew some of those who fished for a living. This is still a primary activity at the Sea of Galilee. Jesus seemed to love this area, as is evidenced by his recurring visits here, his use in teaching of figures of speech related to fishing, and even his resurrected return here as reported by John (John 21:1-24).

This event of the massive catch of fish at the second effort as directed by Jesus appears in John's account as a post-Resurrection event (John 21:4-8). One possible interpretation of the event in John's account is that it is a second episode of the same experience. The reason that the disciples recognized Jesus in the story in John could have been because it brought back their memories of the similar experience that they had had before, as recorded by Luke. In any event, it is interesting to note that the unusual event appears in the Gospel accounts at both the beginning and ending of Jesus' ministry.

Again Jesus' primary focus on a teaching ministry is narrated as he even taught the people from the boat.

Much of the fishing was done at night due to the heat of the day and the fish being at greater depths at that time for that reason. So Simon says, *We have worked all night* . . . (verse 5). Also for this reason it would have been all the more unexpected and surprising to make a sizable catch of fish in the warmth of the day.

Simon felt he was a *sinful man* (verse 8) because he had

had no faith and trust in Jesus' directions or knowledge. Jesus possessed the divine empowerment, which he had witnessed not only on this occasion but at the previous occasion of the healing of his mother-in-law (4:38-39).

Verse 10 is the first mention of two other disciples, James and John, fishing partners with Simon.

Catching *people* (verse 10) would be a higher form of fishing, again at Jesus' direction, which would be required for success. The amazing impression and attraction of Jesus is evident in the response that *they left everything and followed him* (verse 11).

Ministry and Meditation (5:12-16)

Leprosy (verse 12) is a skin disease that results in white hair and raw flesh. Victims of this disease were excluded from the community and also considered ritually unclean. Because they were hopeless and isolated, the urgent yearning of this man for some help is reflected in his falling on his face and *begging* for care, which is what the Greek word also means. The empathy of Jesus for the hurt and isolation of this person is reflected in his stretching *out his hand* and touching him (verse 13).

Leviticus 14:1-32 contains the various examinations and offerings prescribed for one cleansed, or healed, of this disease. Jesus instructed the healed man to follow through on these directives (verse 14).

Once again a pattern emerges, already evident, which Jesus now practiced: the swing back and forth between total involvement with the needs of people to total detachment to meet his own needs (verse 16). After dealing with *crowds gathered to hear,* he withdrew to the wilderness for the third recorded time (4:1, 42).

§ § § § § § §

The Message of Luke 4:14–5:16

Within these verses that describe the beginnings of the ministry of Jesus are found traits that help us sense what was important to Jesus personally and what directions he would take.

We see Jesus' need for spiritual receptivity and replenishment. He obtained this from two sources: corporate worship within his religious tradition and personal, private withdrawal for prayer and pondering. He stood both within his tradition and beyond his tradition. He did not forsake what he inherited, but he also sought and was open to what was beyond it.

Another trait was his willingness and determination to put hands and feet to faith experience. His faith perspective moved him to witness and to caring.

Then the caring took the form of reaching out to those whom society rejected or from whom society stood aloof. Traditional barriers, stigmas, and prejudices were given no heed. Jesus bypassed them and placed human need above traditional distance and rejection. His empathy was strongest for those who received little of such.

Jesus urged his hearers, ancient and modern, to be always open to new possibilities—in achievements and persons. In many times and ways he called upon us to let down our nets again to find marvelous possibilities amidst the improbable.

By his therapeutic helpfulness to those victimized by diseases of mind and/or body, he clearly witnessed to the newly discovered fact that God is on the side of health, not illness. The healing that Jesus brought is an evidence of what God wills and works for humanity, up to our openness to receive and the limits of our mortality.

§ § § § § § §

LUKE 5:17–6:11

Introduction to These Verses

One of the fundamental controversies Jesus would experience begins to surface in this portion of Luke's account. While we have noted that Jesus showed respect for his Jewish heritage and traditions, we sense that he wished to bring new light to that tradition. We wait to see how he would interface the old and the new. This section of the Gospel will begin to show us the nature of the relationship between the two.

Included are events of healing and activities that were exposed to a critique by the religious authorities of the Jewish tradition, and Jesus' own critique of his actions and intentions. The old and the new meet here in the following areas:
   I. Regarding Forgiveness (5:17-32)
  II. Regarding Fasting (5:33-35)
 III. Regarding Attitudes Toward the New (5:36-39)
  IV. Regarding the Sabbath (6:1-11)

Regarding Forgiveness (5:17-32)

We now meet the Pharisees for the first time (verse 17) as Jesus continued teaching. The teacher of the gospel confronted *teachers of the law*, called *scribes*. *Pharisee* comes from an Aramaic word meaning *separated*. They were one of the chief Jewish groups (somewhat similar to what we know as denominations). Among their central concerns were rigid obedience to the law, continuation of ritual traditions, and religious purity through separation in life-style and relationships.

Among the Pharisees as a group were certain persons charged with the responsibility of teaching and interpreting the law in addition to priests who carried out the ritual observances. The fact that so many Pharisaic leaders had *come from every village of Galilee and Judea and from Jerusalem* indicates, on the one hand, the widening impact of Jesus, and on the other hand the spreading curiosity and concern among Jewish leadership. The presence of such a massive crowd in this house (verse 19) adds to this indication.

Residences in Palestine, when not tents, were built with flat roofs. This rooftop area was accessible by a stairway on the outside of the house, usually thin but strong enough to support weight. The roof served as a patio or porch would for us. Thus the companions of the paralytic could go easily to the roof to gain access to the center of the house. The *bed* (NRSV; NIV-*mat*) would be more like a pallet or thin mattress that lay on the floor of a house.

Jesus' proclamation of forgiveness (verse 20) to the paralytic arose out of the early concept of the religious tradition that to be sick was to be "unclean" and that sickness could be the result of sin. This triggered the critical inquiries of the Pharisees, who felt that God alone could forgive. Thus to offer forgiveness was to assume the role of God. This would be blasphemy (verse 21; see Leviticus 24:16). In response, Jesus demonstrated his spiritual authority (verse 24) by declaring the patient healed and directing him to walk. He left, offering the highest gratitude to God, as did those who observed (verses 25-26).

Tax collectors (verse 27) were known to be corrupt, keeping sizable sums collected for themselves. Jesus, like John the Baptist (3:12-13), saw spiritual potential in all persons and would not allow societal prejudice to block him from relating to them. So Jesus went to him, and he followed Jesus, leaving lesser loyalties, rising to a new quality of life, and following new priorities (verse 28). While no one named *Levi* is identified anywhere as one of the Twelve, Matthew identifies himself as a tax collector (Matthew 9:9-12) and relates his own calling to have been like that of Levi. Mark identifies Levi as the *son of Alphaeus* (Mark 2:14). Whether or not Levi and Matthew were the same person is left to conjecture, although it is strongly presumed.

In dining with Levi at a feast (verse 29) possibly paid for out of corrupt income, Jesus incurred strong criticism from the Pharisees and scribes (verse 30). They saw this action as a violation of spiritual separatism and righteousness implied in the law. Jesus saw human need and potential as of greater import than legal righteousness (verse 31).

Regarding Fasting (5:33-35)

Fasting was a spiritual discipline associated with persons of special dedication to God. It was not required by law but was used at times as a means of focusing totally on God and seeking to rise above all physical feelings or yearnings. Moses had practiced such (see Exodus 34:28; Deuteronomy 9:18), as had Elijah, the prophet (1 Kings 19:8). Fasting was also requested of groups of persons as a form of spiritual concentration, intercession, and commitment, such as Jehoshaphat (2 Chronicles 20:3), Ezra (Ezra 8:21), and Esther (Esther 4:16).

Eating and drinking, or feasting, was the opposite of fasting. It contained the notes of celebration and joy. It was also part of Jewish social and religious life. The first feasts recorded in the Bible were carried out by Abraham at the weaning of Isaac (Genesis 21:8) and by Laban at the marriage of Jacob (Genesis 29:22). The Jews who fasted in support of Esther's intercession for their lives feasted when the decree was issued for their protection (Esther

8:17). The ritual festivals prescribed by the law that were times of thanksgiving for past events had feasts as a part of the ritual (for example, the feast of Unleavened Bread, feast of Pentecost or Weeks, and the feast of Tabernacles.)

Thus two forms of spiritual devotion were in contrast among the followers of John the Baptist (verse 33) and Jesus. Here recall that Jesus had just come from a *great banquet* at Levi's house (verse 29). In effect, Jesus affirmed the value of both forms of spiritual observance and expression, suggesting that neither one nor the other is to be used continuously as the only or primary form of spiritual expression. Circumstances rather than custom should suggest the mood and forms of spiritual expression. For the new followers of Jesus, feasting or celebration was the natural expression of their new discovery. But the time would come (verse 35) when apparent separation would find its natural expression in fasting. His comment is in the spirit of Ecclesiastes 3:4.

Regarding Attitudes Toward the New (5:36-39)

There are two versions of the parable in verse 36. Note also Mark's account, which speaks of the old garment being damaged when the new addition to it shrinks (Mark 2:21). In Luke's account both garments are damaged by the transfer of the new piece to the old.

When newly created wine would be placed in a wineskin, fermentation would take place (verse 37). This would expand the wine and further stretch the wineskin at the risk of cracking it.

In both parables Jesus is pointing out the difficulty and risk of intermingling new with old. Yet we must have the new, even if it requires a totally new framework of attitude and understanding to accept it.

Regarding the Sabbath (6:1-11)

Sabbath observance was very precisely defined and described in Jewish law. At the center of those provisions was the third of the Ten Commandments (Exodus 20:8-11; Deuteronomy 5:12-15). This was repeated and amplified at other places in the law (see Exodus 23:12). The effect of these provisions was that no reaping of corn was to take place on the sabbath, regardless of the purpose, since that would be considered "work." Additionally, there was a provision that while plucking grain from a neighbor's field was permitted, putting a sickle to that grain was not permitted at any time (Deuteronomy 23:25). From the Pharisaic viewpoint (verse 2), picking the grains and *rubbing them in their hands* for the purpose of threshing them, as the disciples did (verse 1), was work.

In response, Jesus pointed to another part of the tradition, found in 1 Samuel 21:1-6. When David was fleeing from Saul, he sought food from a priest. The only food available was the sacred Bread of the Presence used in worship. Yet the priest responded to David's request, giving David and his men this bread to eat. Jesus recalled this story to demonstrate that meeting human need took precedence over strict legal obedience.

Here appears (verse 5) for the first time in Luke's account the title *Son of man*. This was a well-known title for the messiah who would come in human form.

By giving attention to how Jesus and his disciples observed the sabbath, the religious heirarchy could determine whether or not Jesus was faithful to the tradition. So Jesus was again observed on a sabbath (Verse 7) when he offered a healing ministry. Jesus turned back on his inquirers their own tradition by asking them whether *good or harm* (NRSV; NIV-*evil*) to *save life or destroy it* is more in keeping with the spirit of the sabbath (verse 9).

The confrontations, and perhaps jealousies, are increasing, carrying a somber note into the future.

§ § § § § § §

The Message of Luke 5:17–6:11

Up to this point in Luke's narrative Jesus has appeared
to be in harmony with the inherited Jewish tradition.
Also he has received wide acclaim and devotion.
Basically, all has been positive.

Now the atmosphere about Jesus changes somewhat.
For one thing, his acclaim becomes a mixed blessing. It
draws attention to him from the religious authorities.
Their attention becomes curiosity, then suspicion, then
jealousy, then resentment, then hostility. And the die is
cast that will ultimately lead to a cross upon a
skull-shaped hill.

All is well until Jesus begins to be, or think, differently
or independently. Jesus never seeks to condemn or
repudiate the law. He shows it both respect and a high
degree of allegience. Yet he sees beyond the law itself in
the purposes of God for persons as revealed through the
law. This is the new thing which Jesus brings.

Jesus seeks to be faithful to both what has been and
what should be. He probably knows well that only time
and the Holy Spirit will lead his hearers then, and now,
to distinguish what is of passing interest as over against
what is of eternal purpose in our spiritual heritage and
experience. This comes as we *grow in the grace and knowledge
of our Lord and Savior Jesus Christ* (2 Peter 3:18), for Jesus
came *among us . . . full of grace and truth* (John 1:14).

§ § § § § § §

PART SIX

LUKE 6:12-49

Introduction to These Verses

As this section begins we observe the specific calling of an inner circle of followers to be known as "disciples" or "apostles" and later referred to as "the Twelve." Following this selection process, Jesus taught some basic guidelines to those persons, along with a sizable number of other followers and a *multitude* of persons curious or seeking assistance. These teachings are a briefer form of a set of teachings recorded in Matthew 5–7 and known familiarly as the Sermon on the Mount. These teachings expand the new perspectives on attitudes and actions that Jesus, as God's spokesman, wished to bring.

The foci of the section are as follows:
   I. A Selected and Receptive Audience (6:12-19)
  II. The Nature of Happiness (6:20-26)
 III. The Nature of Relationships (6:27-42)
 IV. The Tests for Sincerity (6:43-49)

A Selected and Receptive Audience (6:12-19)

Luke again points out the twofold pattern of Jesus: involvement and withdrawal (verse 12). Now for the fourth specific occasion in his account (4:1, 42; 5:16) Jesus has gone to a private place *to pray*. The fact that he spent *all night* in prayer suggests an intensity of feeling or concern. It heightens the sense that something crucial was on his mind and something important was about to happen. That something important was the selection of his inner circle of disciples.

The word *disciple* appears first in Luke's account in 5:30 when it is noted that Pharisees were becoming discontented with them and their fellowship with *sinners*. The word *disciple* (verse 13) means one who is a learner about something, or someone, to which he or she has a commitment. It is not just learning, but learning with a purpose in mind. The number of followers who were moving from curiosity to devotion to commitment as disciples was increasing steadily (verses 17-19).

The reason for Jesus selecting twelve is not given, except the implication that this was a result of prayer. Perhaps Jesus now needed an intimate support group to be companions and assistants and to whom he could impart in some detail the essence of his revelation. Upon them he would have to depend for help now and continuance of witness after his death. They were given the title *apostles*, which is the Greek word meaning *send out*. Mark 3:14-15 identifies the purpose of their calling: *to be with him, and to be sent out to preach and have authority to cast out demons* (3:15). In the early church others would be designated as apostles, such as Paul (Romans 1:1).

Of the twelve listed (verses 14-16) Luke has previously mentioned Simon (4:38-39; 5:4-11), James and John (5:10), and Matthew, if he is the same person as Levi (5:27-29). (Indeed, Levi is called to follow Jesus in that account.) Note that there were two different persons named Simon (verses 14-15) and two different persons named Judas (verse 16). This is often overlooked. Use of *the Zealot* (verse 15) with one of the Simons probably was a nickname, since the revolutionary party by this name did not appear until A.D. 66, unless he became a founder or hero for that movement. The first person named Judas is called Thaddeus in Mark 3:18. *Iscariot* beside the second Judas meant that he was from the village of Kerioth in southern Judea. This list, omitting Judas Iscariot, appears also in Acts 1:13.

Jesus came down and was among the others as an equal *on a level place* (verse 17). Thus in Luke the sermon that followed was given from a plateau in the hills (verse 12). The distance from southern Judea in the south to Sidon on the north coast was about 100 miles. So the multitude came great distances to *hear him and to be healed*.

The Nature of Happiness (6:20-26)

In contrast to the nine beatitudes which appear in Matthew's account (Matthew 5:3-11), Luke records four (verses 20-22). They are shorter or more direct than in Matthew's rendering. The Greek word translated *blessed* also may be translated *happy*. The word in earlier Greek literature was often used to refer to the gods or those who had died. Thus it speaks of a state of blessedness or happiness beyond ordinary human experience.

The beatitudes in Luke's rendering may have been in their original form, expanded or reinterpreted later by Matthew. Four categories of human experience are identified with empathy: the poor, the hungry, the sad, the persecuted and/or rejected. This helps us to discover those for whom Jesus had special concern. The statements were stunning because they suggested that those who usually seemed to be the most unhappy because of their plight could actually become the happiest because of how God would meet their needs.

On the other side, Jesus suggested that those who seemed to have all that others thought they would want for their happiness may, after all, become the unhappiest. Four *woes* are given by Luke to match the blessings (verses 24-26). They appear in no other Gospel account. To get their impact, read the following combinations: verse 20b and verse 24; verse 21a and verse 25a; verse 21b and verse 25b; verse 22 and verse 26. You will immediately see the unusual paradoxes Jesus was proclaiming. They are the oposite of the usual human perspective, and show that the sources of true and lasting happiness must be deeper, and more divine in origin, than momentary pleasures.

This rendering of blessings and woes (or curses) is somewhat in the spirit of Moses' summary to his followers in Deuteronomy 11:26-28.

The Nature of Relationships (6:27-42)

The beginning of verse 27 with *But I say to you . . .* does not fit well grammatically or in flow of thought with the preceding verse. This could mean that something has been omitted here by Luke or a copying scribe. Verse 28 appears in Matthew at 5:44. In that passage, the preceding verse quotes a common attitude: "You shall love your neighbor and hate your enemy." The call to *love your enemies* is in response to that specific attitude or custom. Thus it is possible that this reference to a prevalent attitude is missing here, and perhaps even a larger portion of the sermon.

The Greek word translated *love* in verse 27 is *agape,* the self-giving highest type of love. This type of love we are to show even to our enemies.

These verses on the nature of love (verses 27-36) portray a radically new concept of love, but one which is rooted in the nature and action of God (verse 35). Our model and motivation are not the tendencies of others around us or impulses within us, but the divine spirit flowing to and through us.

In verse 29, *cloak* (NIV; NRSV = *coat*) is an outer garment and *tunic* (NIV; NRSV = *shirt*) is an undergarment.

The so-called Golden Rule appears in verse 31.

The underlying principle called for in the counsel given in verses 32-36 is that love is something to be initiated by us, not simply a response made by us. Jesus' followers are to love not on the basis of love received or expected but as those called to share love regardless of receptivity or consequence. We love not to obtain love, but simply out of the privilege and desire to love. This might correspond to Dietrich Bonhoeffer's concept of "tough love" that is the Christian's calling.

The Greek verb translated expecting nothing in return (verse 35) is a word that appears only at this one place in the entire New Testament. Thus it is an unusual word and difficult to translate because of few places in which the word can be observed.

To be _merciful_ (verse 36) means to be compassionate, with pity toward one another.

The imagery in verse 38 arises out of the ways the grain was harvested. After the wheat was harvested, it was bound together, but then _shaken_ loose in threshing. Then the remaining grain was put into containers filled to capacity, even overfilled. Such grain, put into one's _lap,_ a large pocket, or fold in an outer garment, would be more than the pocket could contain. A generous spirit will find itself to be the recipient of generosity in the same measure, but not necessarily of the same substance.

The statements in verses 39-40 could be called proverbs as much as parables. Perhaps they were familiar proverbs that Jesus quoted because they have valuable truths to teach. (For more extensive comments on parables, see the commentary on 8:4). Jesus, on this occasion, was speaking primarily to his disciples. In the statement about the blind man leading another, Jesus set a sense of direction for a disciple. A disciple must be literally a _learner_ in order to lead. Without spiritual insight or vision, a disciple may lead nowhere, for the disciple knows not where to go. Also the disciple must always perceive that she or he is a learner, but not the teacher (verse 40), until that insight has been obtained from the teacher who is the model.

The humor of Jesus appears in verses 41-42. It is in the contrast he draws between one who is bothered by a _speck_ of sawdust or sliver of wood in another's eye, unaware of an entire log jamming one's own vision. Exaggeration can be a form of humor. Stating a point in impossible terms gets the point across in a memorable way. In a sense, this parable is stating the point made in the statement about the blind men and doing it with another visual image. One must clear up one's own vision before one can clearly see accurately enough to clear up someone else's spiritual vision.

The English word *hypocrite* (verse 42) is an exact rendering of a Greek word with the same spelling. The Greek word means *an actor* and comes from a root word meaning to answer on the stage or play a part. Thus a hypocrite is one who simply acts or plays a part in seeming to be more righteous than others.

The Tests for Sincerity (6:43-49)

The figures of speech were taken out of the commonplace observances in the lives of Jesus' hearers: trees, fruit, figs, bramble bushes, building a house. He used simple, understandable items to unveil divine truths, thus showing his skill as a master teacher.

The saying in verse 43 is related to the insight in verse 42. If there is *bad fruit* emerging from someone's life, it indicates that there is something wrong within (that is, a "log" of evil). If there really is a *good treasure* (verse 45) within, then this *heart* will produce good. It is out of the *overflow* (NIV; NRSV-*abundance*) of the heart that persons give expression. In Jesus' time, the heart was seen not as the seat of feelings but as the center of thinking.

Luke's rendering of the statement in verse 46 is far more personal than Matthew's rendering (see Matthew 7:21). Jesus speaks here of *you* rather than *everyone*. In the preceding teachings, Jesus had unveiled new dimensions and forms of discipleship. Now he called his hearers to move from devotion and adoration (*Lord, Lord*) to authentic discipleship of deeds (*does them*), arising out of the genuinely *good treasure of the heart.* No contrary force could *shake it, because it had been well built* (verse 48).

§ § § § § § §

The Message of Luke 6:12-49

There are really two callings that are found in this section of the Gospel recorded by Luke. The first is the calling of certain persons to a relationship, a special relationship with Christ. This testifies to the importance of persons in the sight of God and the potential of persons in God's plan and strategic service. These persons are not unlike any of us to whom Jesus still calls.

The second calling is to a quality of discipleship which is different, deep, and genuine, informed and shaped by the model of Jesus. This calling also comes to us. If we respond only to the calling into a relationship and falter at the threshold of the second calling, then we never really become his disciples. Our encouragement is that the *power comes forth from him* (verse 19).

§ § § § § § §

Introduction to These Verses

Two highly dramatic miracles of healing occur at the beginning of this chapter: the healing of a Roman centurion's servant and the return to life of a widow's son. The public context of these events is as important as the events themselves, because it spreads even more widely abroad the reputation of Jesus among Gentiles and Jews.

Interestingly, these events indirectly result in John the Baptist reentering the narrative to make some inquiries of Jesus. Then Jesus offers an appraisal of John.

The material falls into three parts:
  I. Impressive Miracles (7:1-17)
 II. John's Query and Jesus' Response (7:18-23)
III. Jesus' Appraisal of John (7:24-35)

Impressive Miracles (7:1-17)

The preceding section appears to have taken place in the Galilee area. The events in this section continue in that region. Capernaum (verse 1) had been visited by Jesus (4:31) shortly after his visit to the synagogue in Nazareth. Thus he was returning for at least a second time to this town on the coast of the Sea of Galilee.

A *centurion* (verse 2) was an officer in the army who originally commanded one hundred soldiers and later in history commanded a large group of soldiers, but not necessarily exactly one hundred. The account implies that he was a not a Jew. Only one other time does Luke record a centurion's action, and that is at the cross after the crucifixion (23:47). In both instances these Roman officers are portrayed as awed and positive toward Jesus.

The Greek word describing the slave as *valued highly* (verse 2) could be translated as *honored, prized,* or *precious.* It is really unclear as to whether the slave was valued for performance or personal attachment by the centurion.

There was an unusual interrelationship between this Roman centurion and the Jewish community (verses 3-5). At first he asked the elders of the Jews, who would be officers of the local synagogue, to approach Jesus in his behalf. So empathetic were they with this Roman that they pled *earnestly* for him, even speaking of his love for their nation and gifts, either through contributions or material and manpower, to their synagogue. There appears here a mutual admiration and support which underlines the tolerance and openness of this officer. Also this seeking out of Jesus for healing help by the centurion points out how widespread and positive was the reputation of Jesus now among non-Jews as well as Jews.

The phrase *I am not worthy* (verse 6, NRSV; NIV = *I do not deserve*) suggests a sense of hesitant humility on the part of the centurion in the presence of Jesus. However, this sentence can be translated in a way that suggests the centurion felt it was inappropriate for Jesus to come into his home. This could have been because of his fear that it might damage Jesus' image among Jews to be in a Roman officer's home. Or the Roman officer might have feared what other Romans would say about him seeking the presence and ministry of Jesus.

The centurion fell back on a military model (verses 7-8), asking of Jesus not his presence but his order only for healing to take place. Since the centurion was a person of authority whom others had to obey, he presumed Jesus to have the same type of spiritual authority. Again, this manifested the high appraisal of Jesus by the centurion. So striking was it that Jesus himself marvelled, feeling that such faith and confidence exceeded that to be found among his own national community (verse 9).

Faith and expectation were linked to the healing process as the intercessors returned home and, indeed, found the slave healed (verse 10) without the personal visit and touch of Jesus.

Nain (verse 11) is about 25-30 miles south of Capernaum and five or six miles southeast of Nazareth. It is near the border of Samaria. The name means *pleasant* because of the lovely view there of the Plain of Esdraelon.

What Jesus encountered was a funeral procession moving out of the town gate (verse 12) toward a burial area, probably just outside the gate (as the cemetery at Jerusalem was located just outside the city walls).

A *widow* (verse 12) could be identified by special clothing worn (see Genesis 38:14, 19). The Jewish law included a priority concern for the widowed (see Exodus 22:22; Deuteronomy 14:29; 24:17-21; 26:12-13). The Old Testament tradition revealed God to be the champion of the rights and welfare of the widowed and fatherless (see Deuteronomy 10:18; Psalm 68:5; Isaiah 1:17; Jeremiah 7:6; 22:3; Zechariah 7:10; Malachi 3:5). Thus Jesus' concern for this widow's plight would be a natural outgrowth and expression of his own spiritual tradition. This particular event was even more traumatic because the widow had lost her *only son* (verse 12) as well as her husband. This meant she has lost her family identity and continuity, leaving her alone socially and economically.

Of the three synoptic Gospels, only in Luke is Jesus called *Lord* (verse 13). This title really came into widespread usage in the early church as a part of their worship liturgies. The Greek word translated *compassion* (NRSV; NIV = *his heart went out*) meant a loud expression of pain or sorrow, especially for the dead. It could be translated *to weep* or *lament*. In a sense, it meant identifying with another's hurt through one's own tears. While entering thus into the widow's own hurt, he said, *Do not weep.*

A *bier* (verse 14) is a *coffin* or a container for a dead body.

Fear (verse 16, NRSV; NIV = *awe*) as used here really means a deep awe or reverence. Once again, to glorify God means to offer the highest praise and gratitude.

To see Jesus as *a great prophet* (verse 16) means to see him as one who indeed *speaks for* God. The second affirmation makes this even clearer: *God has visited his people!*

Since this event took place in Galilee, for the word to *spread throughout Judea* (verse 17) meant that it moved through Samaria down to Judea. This really meant that the report had spread throughout the entire Jewish nation.

John's Query and Jesus' Response (7:18-23)

This same report had reached even to John the Baptist (verse 18) in the wilderness areas of Judea. John had been separated by distance from the areas where Jesus had been ministering. He had not personally witnessed that ministry. Presumably, he had not seen Jesus since the baptism. Now, hearing increasing rumors and reports of that ministry, John decided to make inquiries for himself by sending representatives to Jesus. John may also have surmised that his future and life might be in danger. If so, he may have wanted to receive the assurance that his hopes and predictions had come to pass. Possibly John may have had some of the same expectations of earlier generations for a messiah appearing as a political or military liberator. Jesus was not moving in that direction. Was Jesus the messiah or not?

The question in verse 20 may be a question as to

whether or not Jesus was the messiah, or whether Jesus was Elijah returned as prophesied. The response to John by Jesus in verse 22 is another way of saying what Jesus had taught in 6:43-44. The *good fruit* of his ministry should speak for itself.

Jesus' Appraisal of John (17:24-35)

The heart of Jesus' appraisal of John the Baptist is in verse 26: *A prophet . . . and more than a prophet.* This was no small compliment because it meant that Jesus saw in John an authentic spokesperson for God. Prophets were known for the rigor of their lifestyles and messages, holding allegiance only to God and finding their messages only from God (*Thus says the Lord . . .*). Understanding Jesus' recognition of John's status, we can better understand the preceding dialogue. A prophet stood steady in conviction, nor blown about by every wind of influence or enticement. A prophet knew sacrifice of comfort and popularity, not luxury and kingly privilege.

The quotation in verse 27 is from Malachi 3:1. By quoting this reference, Jesus identified John as God's special messenger to prepare the way for the messiah. This is what is meant by *more than a prophet.*

Verse 28 is a strange statement. It appears to give to John the highest accolade and yet a startling put-down. The implication was that with the coming of Jesus a new spiritual era had dawned. With the discoveries and experiences to be had in this new kingdom-awareness, their spiritual legacy would far exceed anything known or achieved earlier, as great as that was. That was the time only of promise; this was the time of actuality.

The reaction of those who heard this appraisal varied. Those baptized by John felt that God was just (*acknowledged that God's way was right,* verse 29), since in mercy God had come to them with new possibilities for their lives. The Pharisees, however, *rejected* (verse 30) Jesus' interpretation of John's spiritual role and the new Kingdom now among them.

Jesus now reacted to the reactions of the Pharisees. What

was obvious did not produce what should be the obvious results. Indeed, the opposite results occurred. Jesus here may have been quoting a popular saying (verse 32). The reactions of the Pharisees to both John and Jesus have been the opposite of what should have taken place. Although obviously showing his dedication to God through self-discipline, John was seen to be demonic (verse 33). Jesus simply moved into the commonplace experiences and relationships of life to bring God's presence to both, but was criticized as one who had lost commitment and self-control (recall also 5:30).

Wisdom is proved right by all her children (verse 35) means that the future brings the experience to know accurately who is right or wrong. Time will tell.

§ § § § § § §

The Message of Luke 7:1-35

Caring and conviction are evident in this chapter. We see not only two dramatic episodes of healing, but repeated new references to the outreach ministries of Jesus. Then occurs a significant declaration and witness: The mark of God's special servant is not military or political power, but love in action through caring. This attitude identifies those who are indeed God's people or Jesus' disciples. It is not so much what is proclaimed in God's name but what is shared of one's self to meet others' needs in God's name that marks the lifestyle of a disciple.

Additionally, there is the importance of conviction. The spiritual conviction and sacrifice of John the Baptist is identified and admired. Jesus goes on to express his own conviction related to where truth lies, and how spiritual sophisticates can still miss the truth God lays at their doorsteps. Informed conviction must stand even though it is rejected or ridiculed.

§ § § § § § §

LUKE 7:36–9:17

Introduction to These Chapters

Jesus' ministry moved into ever-widening circles of expression and expectation. More demands were placed upon him; more persons were exposed to him; more reactions took place around him. As he continued his expanding ministry of deed and word, he also began to interpret the nature of the relationship between his gospel and the world of people and powers around him. He both discussed and modeled what it meant to be in the world but not of the world.

This section develops as follows.
   I. Gratitude of the Forgiven (7:36-8:3)
  II. The Word Sown in the World (8:4-18)
 III. The Wider Family of Jesus (8:19-21)
 IV. The Mastery of Christ (8:22-56)
      A. Mastery over physical elements (8:22-39)
      B. Mastery over disease and death (8:40-56)
  V. Commission to Minister to the World (9:1-6)
 VI. Lingering Recollection of John (9:7-9)
VII. Sensitivity to Physical Need (9:10-17)

Gratitude of the Forgiven (7:36-8:3)

Note that although the *Pharisees* (verse 36) had been critical of him, Jesus still went to dine with them. He took the initiative to bridge gaps. He would not allow their prejudice toward him to prevent his coming to them. His host's name was Simon, the third different person by that name encountered so far in Luke's account (see 4:38; 6:15).

The woman is identified as a sinner (verse 37). The original Greek word means *one who has missed the mark.* In Jewish usage it would mean one who is disobedient to the law and commandments. In using this description of her, Luke expressed the widespread attitude toward her by the people of the area. She was not seen in terms of her name, vocation, family status, or residence—only as *a sinner.*

A Jewish woman often carried a small alabaster container of perfume around her neck. This frequently was one of her most valuable possessions. Her unbound hair would have been a sign of immodesty. The marriage tradition called for a girl to bind up her hair on her wedding day and never again appear in public with it unbound.

It was the custom for persons to remove their sandals upon entering a home. Thus Jesus would be dining with his feet uncovered. it was also customary for the host to arrange for the washing of the roadway dust from a guest's feet as an expression of hospitality. Anointing the body with olive oil was done after bathing and also used to smooth the hair. It was also offered as an expression of hospitality. For some reason, these had not been arranged by Simon, nor had Jesus even been greeted with the usual kiss of welcome (verse 45). So in kissing his feet, using perfume to bathe and anoint them, and wiping them with her hair, this unknown woman of poor reputation expressed both customary courtesy and uncommon devotion.

A *prophet* (verse 39) would have been a person of spiritual understanding and vision, thus knowing the sinful reputation of this person. Her *touching* him in public would have been a mark of shame and the spreading of ceremonial uncleanness.

Denarii (verse 41) were a type of currency. Each denarius would be worth about one-fourth of a cent in present United States currency, but had much more value then.

An interesting new understanding of forgiveness comes in verse 48. Being aware of her own great spiritual need and her own lack of merit, she used this awareness to stimulate her to reach out to others in need, not for merit but out of empathy. Instead of self-despair, she was led to service. For this reason Jesus described her as *forgiven* (verse 48). In being loved we find our own needs met. This is the essence of love. But if we have no awareness of need within ourselves, then we may well not have sensitivity to the deep needs of others. Thus the one who is *forgiven little, loves little* (verse 47).

The theme of the *kingdom of God* (8:1) continued to be central in the preaching of Jesus.

Women also were among the close followers of Jesus, sometimes out of gratitude for his empathy with them and deliverance to them. Mary Magdalene was Mary of Magdalia, a town on the southwest coast of the Sea of Galilee. By some she is thought to be the woman described earlier in this section who anointed Jesus and was forgiven. There is no proof of this.

A *steward* (verse 3, NRSV; NIV = *manager*) was an administrator of business matters for the king, this king being Herod Antipas. Joanna (*God has been gracious*) and Susanna (*a lily*) are named only in Luke's account. These women shared what they had to provide for the needs of the Twelve.

The Word Sown in the World (8:4-18)

The parable of the sower gives a picture of the ways in which the Gospel was, and would be, received by the world. All the figures of speech in this parable—sower, birds, rock, no moisture, thorns, good soil (verses 5-8)—were well-known and encountered by everyone in his audience. They knew the riskiness of farming in a land of rocky, arid soil. Of all seed sown, only a small amount would actually take root and grow because of the rocks, the birds, the weeds or thorns, and the drought. What little might take root would probably bring forth a sizable amount.

Jesus had previously made use of parables in Luke's account (see 5:36-39; 6:39-44; 7:41-43). This method of teaching will be increasingly used as his account continues.

A parable is a picture story used to convey insight. It differs from an allegory in that the story as a whole conveys that message rather than each specific component or character being representative of something or someone. It differs from a metaphor in that it is more expansive than just a figure of speech and usually involves some action or sequence of events.

The parables as developed by Jesus were always lifted out of or made up of characters and events easily identifiable in the everyday lives of his hearers. This was a part of his genius as a teacher, using the commonplace to teach uncommon truth.

The net effect of the puzzling statement in verse 10 is, first of all, to indicate that there are *secrets* of the Kingdom which are only really understood by those who have a faith perspective born out of their discipleship and spiritual insights. They can see and hear spiritual truth that simply passes others by. A simple story can unveil God's ways to them, while to others it is only a simple story. Faith opens our eyes and discipleship makes us sensitive. Yet for those outside this spiritual realm, *seeing they may not see, and hearing they may not understand* (verse 10, NIV).

The explanation of the parable by Jesus is striking in its simplicity and clarity (verses 11-15). He tells us all we need to know.

A *lamp* (verse 16) was essential for illumination in a residence of that day and place. For a lamp to be hidden away would destroy its reason for being and burning.

The comment in verse 17 may relate back to verse 10. Whereas there has been a time when only those within the circle of faith and faithfulness clearly perceived the truth, in time these secrets will become obvious to all. Another paradox is stated in verse 18. Those who have the truth will find more truth. Those who have made little room for the truth may lose what faith or insight they have.

The Wider Family of Jesus (8:19-21)

This is the first reference to Mary, the mother of Jesus, since his emergence into adulthood. Matthew identified four brothers of Jesus: James, Joseph, Simon, and Judas (Matthew 13:55). James later became head of the church at Jerusalem after the Christian movement was initiated by the Resurrection and experience of the Holy Spirit (Acts 12:17; 15:13; 21:18; Galatians 1:19; 2:9, 12). The other brothers are not mentioned elsewhere in Scripture.

The fact that the mother and brothers of Jesus could not reach him *for the crowd* (verse 19) suggests that they were not known by many, if any, of the followers of Jesus, and had not been with him often.

Jesus expanded the concept of his family to include those who were faithful children of God. These became as close as kin in his spiritual sense of community.

Mastery over Physical Elements (8:22-39)

The *lake* (verse 22) is again the Sea of Galilee. A storm such as what is described here is not unusual on this body of water. The sea is surrounded by hills in a setting much like a cup. Wind currents passing over the area suddenly descend, after crossing over the hills, to the sea level. These forceful winds stir up strong currents and storms on short notice.

This episode of Jesus and the storm at sea is one of a limited number of events that are recorded in all four Gospel accounts. Previously, disease and death were seen as subject to the power of Jesus. Added to that now are the physical elements of the universe that are subject to his power. *He commands even the winds and the water, and they obey him* (verse 25).

Gerasenes refers to persons living in an area on the east shore of the Sea of Galilee near a site called Gerasa or Gadara (in some translations the residents are called *Gadarenes*).

For information on demon-possession, see the commentary on 4:33-36. This man suffered the symptoms of a loss of dignity and self-control (wore *no clothes,* verse 27) and was rejected by the community (lived *in the tombs*). This mentally ill man had been so tormented by those around him that he feared Jesus would also *torment* him. The treatment method had been to bind him *with chains and shackles* (verse 29, NRSV; NIV = *hand and foot*), which served the purpose of a modern-day straitjacket.

A *legion* (verse 30) was a military term for a huge army division, numbering in the thousands. The patient considered himself filled with multiple personalities and destructive forces.

The happenings recorded in verses 31-35 are puzzling to us. The stampede of pigs which occurred at this point may have been a coincidence, or they may have been frightened by the ill man's actions. In any event, the destruction of the swine suggests the destructive power of the evil forces from which *Legion* had been set free.

The response of the residents of the area to the healed man is striking. *They were afraid* (verse 35). They were so afraid of Legion when he was ill that they bound him and rejected him from the community. Now he was well, and so different from before that they were still afraid. Furthermore, the radical transformation of Legion, the destructive stampede of the swine, and the perception of evil forces all around left all the residents of the area in *great fear* (verse 37). Out of fear they made the one person leave who had brought sanity to their section. Legion realized that he had met one person who understood him, and thus he wanted to go with the man. Yet he was sent back home to witness about his experience.

62

Mastery over Disease and Death (8:40-56)

The place to which Jesus *returned* is not given, but was the place he left in verse 22, probably Capernaum.
A *ruler of the synagogue* was one of the male elders or lay officials of the local place of Jewish worship (verse 41).

The *woman* had a chronic condition of internal bleeding, perhaps a constant menstrual flow. Mark 5:26 describes this woman as one *who had endured much under many physicians* (NRSV). Interestingly, Luke, a physician, omits this phrase in his account.

She *came up behind him* (verse 44), very possibly because under the law her condition made her ceremonially unclean (see Leviticus 15:25-30), and thus isolated from the stream of community and religious life and robbed of personal pride.

The fringe (NRSV; NIV-*edge*) of his garment probably refers to one of the four tassels of white thread with a blue thread woven through them attached to the edge (or fringe) of the outer garment worn by every devout Jew. These tassels were prescribed by Jewish law (Numbers 15:38-39; Deuteronomy 22:12) to serve as reminders to be obedient to the commandments. One end of the garment was hung over the shoulder with a tassel that could have been touched by someone approaching from behind.

Falling down *before him* (verse 47) may have been an act of fear more than worship, since she was *trembling*. An unclean person was not to touch another person, lest that person be made unclean also.

Go in peace was a familiar benediction in the Old Testament tradition (see 1 Samuel 1:17; 29:7). "Peace," or "Shalom" is a great keynote of that tradition. To this woman, who had been robbed of peace by her physical ailment, Jesus was now saying that, by virtue of the healing she had experienced, she would be able to go back into the mainstream of Jewish life and worship with a new sense of spiritual and emotional well-being, or peace.

Jesus is again referred to as *the teacher* (verse 49; see

also 7:40). This seems to be the prevailing image that Jesus had created about himself at this time.

For the first time in Luke's account *Peter, John, and James* (verse 51) were chosen to accompany Jesus as an inner circle of disciples to be with Jesus on certain special occasions.

The return of the child's *spirit* (verse 55) brought life. There was a differentiation between body and spirit. The body would die because the spirit left the body and went to Sheol. Thus the only way her body could return to life would be for her spirit to return to the body.

Commission to Minister to the World (9:1-6)

Now the Twelve moved from just being learners to become doers. When Jesus gave them *power and authority* over *all demons and to cure diseases* (9:1), he enabled and stimulated them to be in mission. Their mission had been modeled by Jesus himself. The Twelve were to do what Jesus had been doing, and had just done (8:26-48). They were also to preach what Jesus had been preaching: the *kingdom of God* (verse 2). Their twofold mission was *to preach* and *to heal,* to witness always by both the spoken word and the caring therapeutic act.

The verb translated *sent them out* is the Greek word *apostello,* from which *apostle* comes. (See the commentary on Luke 6:13.) Thus the ones to be *sent out* were now being sent out.

A *staff* (verse 3) was a walking stick or shepherd's crook which could be used to assist in climbing uphill or defending oneself from animals. A bag or pack was used to carry one's possessions or traveling articles. *Tunics* were shorts or undergarments. These prohibitions were to the effect that they should travel light, with their movement in mission unhindered by possessions.

The tradition of the rabbis was to shake the dust off their sandals or feet before entering Palestine, if they had passed through Gentile or "pagan" areas. Thus to *shake off the dust* (verse 5) would testify to the pagan nature or blindness of any who rejected the disciples' witness.

The mission to preach and heal was reaffirmed by the Twelve actually doing these things.

Lingering Recollection of John (9:7-9)

Luke does not provide the detailed story of the events leading to the death of John the Baptist that occurs in Mark's account (Mark 6:17-29). This account appears to presume that the readers knew what had happened to John by simply quoting Herod as saying *John is beheaded* (verse 9). (See the commentaries on 3:18-20 and 7:18-35.)

The fact that Herod had *heard of all that had occurred* (verse 7) indicated that by now the reputation of Jesus had come to the attention not only of Jewish officials but also to Roman officials. Herod, because of his violent act against John, feared the spectre of John's reappearing. Listing the rumors also identified the various interpretations current as to the identity of Jesus. The disciple would report the same rumors to Jesus (verse 19). The fact that Herod, the ruler, *tried to see* Jesus was an unexpected development.

Sensitivity to Physical Need (9:10-17)

Verse 10 could read, "On their return the sent-out ones told him what they had done." The apostles also were introduced to the pattern of occasional withdrawal after intense involvement in meeting human need, such as Jesus himself had been practicing (4:1, 42; 5:16). Bethsaida, mentioned here for the first time in Luke's account, is a town in the Gennesaret area east of the Jordan River. The name means *house of the fisher.*

Again in verse 11 the twofold mission is evident: to preach or teach of the *kingdom of God,* and to heal.

This story of the feeding of more than five thousand persons is the only miraculous event which appears in all four Gospel accounts (Matthew 15:32-38; Mark 8:1-9; John

6:1-14). *Loaves* and *fish* (verse 13) were the common food items of the poor in Palestine. They were readily available and easily carried. The record of the way Jesus handled the food items (verse 16) may have been influenced by the early church customs related to the Lord's Supper. There the person presiding took the bread loaf, offered a prayer of thanksgiving and dedication, broke it into smaller pieces, and gave it to assistants or deacons to distribute. It was also a Jewish custom to offer a form of this blessing before every meal: "Blessed art thou, Lord our God, King of the universe, who bringest forth bread from the earth." Looking *up to heaven* was not an uncommon posture for prayer in the Jewish tradition. It was more common than kneeling.

To collect what was *left over* (verse 17) was a common practice. By describing *baskets* of leftovers, the miraculous nature of the event was being emphasized. The use of twelve baskets may mean that each of the twelve who had been given a portion of the loaves and fish brought back a basket of leftovers.

§ § § § § § §

The Message of Luke 7:36–9:17

This section unveils for us a Christ who moves out into the world, motivated and directed by the desire and intention to meet human need. The need may be the need for forgiveness, new insight into truth, a sense of belonging, hope amidst fear, release from the demonic, healing for illness, or life amid death. Human need becomes the magnet for Jesus' ministry.

And it is the same for all his disciples, ancient and modern. To believe in Christ is to become his disciple—and to join his mission to witness and to heal!

§ § § § § § §

LUKE 9:18-50

Introduction to These Verses

This section comes midway in the narrative account of Jesus' ministry prior to the triumphal entry into Jerusalem. It immediately follows the feeding of the multitude (9:12-17), which must have created both awe and curiosity. Jesus' reputation as a teacher and miracle worker had become widespread. So it would have been natural for many to be asking one another, and themselves, what even Herod had asked: *Who is this about whom I hear such things?* (verse 9).

Aware of these questions, Luke attempts now to provide some explicit answers by bringing into his account some events that testify to the nature of Christ. The following themes appear in and through these events.

   I. Messiahship Affirmed and Interpreted (9:18-22)
  II. Implications for Discipleship (9:23-27)
 III. Exaltation and Validation of Christ (9:28-36)
 IV. Evidence of Messiahship (9:37-45)
  V. Redefining Greatness and Community (9:46-50)

Messiahship Affirmed and Interpreted (9:18-22)

One more time Jesus had withdrawn with the disciples to a private place (verse 18) after a demanding public involvement—feeding the multitude. Since this is the fifth withdrawal experience recorded by Luke, it is obvious that this pattern both impressed Luke and was deemed important by him.

There was a movement in Jesus' questions from the general to the personal. He began rather objectively in a non-threatening manner by asking for a report from his disciples as to what opinion they had heard from *the crowds* about who he was (verse 18). Then he turned to the personal inquiry of them as to who they said he was (verse 20).

The response of the disciples to the first question echoed the rumors which were being reported to Herod (see 9:7-8). (Regarding the expectation of Elijah's return, see the commentary on 1:17.) The fact that Jesus was seen as possibly *one of the prophets* (verse 19) suggested how widely he was seen as being in the tradition of the Old Testament prophets—the Lord's spokesperson.

Christ (verse 20, NIV; NRSV = *Messiah*) is a rendering of the Greek word *christos*, which literally means an *anointed one*. It is the word used for the Hebrew word *messiah*. Thus the two words are interchangeable.

After Peter's strong affirmation of Jesus as God's messiah, the old inherited messianic images and hopes might have appeared in the minds of the hearers. Those images were of a person of military might and political supremacy or rulership. Sensitive to those expectations, Jesus immediately sought to correct the expectations after Peter's identification of Jesus as Messiah. Although Peter had spoken of Jesus as *Christ of God*, Jesus chose for himself the title emphasizing his human aspect, *Son of man* (verse 22). Then he spoke of suffering, rejection, and death rather than acclaim. This must have been a shock for Peter and the others.

Implications for Discipleship (9:23-27)

What Jesus described as being in store for himself became also the job description for his followers. They must enter into self-denial (verse 23), that is, disregarding all thought of themselves, and bear the cross. This is the first specific mention of the cross in Luke. Since it was used for the painful execution of criminals, it must have come across to his hearers as an unbelievably harsh symbol for discipleship.

Verses 24 and 25 express in different forms the same paradox of losing by gaining and gaining by losing.

In verse 26 is the first reference in Luke to the Second Coming. The imagery is very similar to Old Testament prophetic descriptions of the coming of the messiah. Note a similar thought expressed in 1 John 2:28.

The statement in verse 27 might be best read as a sequel to verse 24, which suggests that losing one's life might be a result of discipleship. Verse 27 suggests that even if that happens, evidences of the Kingdom will be seen (not the Kingdom in all its fullness) before death, and they will know that discipleship was not in vain.

Exaltation and Validation of Christ (9:28-36)

Another withdrawal experience occurred for prayer, with this being the first including just Peter, John, and James (verse 28).

The changing or transforming of Jesus' facial features was what gave this locale the name of the Mount of Transfiguration.

Moses was considered the lawgiver and Elijah one of the earliest and greatest of the prophets (verse 30). Thus representatives of the Law and the Prophets appeared with Jesus. This suggested the spiritual greatness of Jesus, that persons of such spiritual stature would appear with him. Also it symbolized Jesus as the fulfillment of and successor to the Law and the Prophets. Only in Luke's account does a reference appear to what these persons discussed (verse 31).

Only in Luke, as well, is there a description of the three disciples being asleep, but waking to witness the gathering (verse 32). This identifies the event as taking place at night.

The word translated *dwellings* or *shelters* (verse 33) could be translated tents or *tabernacles.* It is word that was used as the term for the Mosaic tabernacles. Thus the idea was probably that three tents of worship should be erected, one for each of these spiritual heroes.

In several scriptural events a *cloud* (verse 34) stood for the presence of God (see 1 Kings 8:10, for example). The most famous is the event upon Mount Sinai when Moses encountered a cloud covering the mountain out of which God spoke to him (Exodus 24:15-18). In that event and this event those present *entered the cloud,* or were absorbed into the presence of God. Some see the word-picture as suggesting this mountain experience is a second Sinai in which God spoke out of divine glory to the special servant of the Lord.

Jesus was *chosen* to be the Messiah (verse 35).

The silence (verse 36) of the disciples was in keeping with the concept of a messianic secret. A few would know Jesus was the Messiah but they would hold it as a secret until Jesus chose to reveal that secret to all.

Evidence of Messiahship (9:37-45)

As Jesus moved out of private withdrawal, he again encountered a great *crowd* (verse 37). Back and forth Jesus moved from one to the other in Luke's account.

The description of the child's symptoms is appropriate for an account by physician Luke. The description suggests an attack of epilepsy.

The complaint in verse 41 seems to be in contrast with the general attitude of Jesus. It is somewhat like some Old Testament expressions condemning the faithlessness of God's chosen people. Perhaps it may simply be an expression arising out of the weariness of Jesus.

Strange and bizarre behavior (verse 42) that was

beyond human control was presumed thus to be under demonic control (see the commentary on 4:33-36).

In verse 44 Jesus repeated his sinister warning of what would happen. He did so in the light of the astonishment and marvel of the people after healing the epileptic boy. He did not want his disciples to be deluded by this acclaim into thinking that suffering was not to come. The disciples still could not understand this and harmonized it with what they had observed and felt.

Redefining Greatness and Community (9:46-50)

Once again Jesus used a paradox as a means of teaching after using a child as an object lesson (verses 47-48). This time it was that the least may be the greatest.

Exorcisms were performed by persons of different religious backgrounds in Palestine (verse 49). Jesus here affirmed that the good one does is of more importance than the group to which one belongs.

§ § § § § § §

The Message of Luke 9:18-50

Divinity and humanity are blended in this section. On the one hand we see the highest affirmations about Jesus: *the Christ of God* (verse 20), and *This is my Son—my chosen* (verse 35). We see the astonishment and marvel of the people. We even see the disciples wanting to immerse themselves in this greatness (verse 46).

However, what Jesus tries to unveil is a new definition of divinity. To be God's Son means to enter into the world of God's children. To be glorified means to be called to sacrifice. To be Messiah means to suffer. Unbelievable these concepts were and distasteful they still are. The credentials of divinity are now to be established by servanthood.

§ § § § § § §

PART TEN LUKE 9:51–10:42

Introduction to These Chapters

The location of events now began to shift as Jesus set out *to go to Jerusalem* (9:51). In a sense the atmosphere became more solemn, the teachings more expansive and insistent, and concerns about the future more evident. It was both the end of the beginning and the beginning of the end of Jesus' ministry.

Our first focus relates to the location through which Jesus passed, the area of Samaria and its residents. Then there will also be attention given to the sending out of others in discipleship, as well as a personal visit to the home of friends of Jesus. The outline is as follows.

I. Samaritans Resenting and Resented (9:51-56)
II. Priorities for Discipleship (9:57-62)
III. Sending Out of Emissaries (10:1-24)
IV. The Good Samaritan (10:25-37)
V. Visit with Martha and Mary (10:38-42)

Samaritans Resenting and Resented (9:51-56)

What appears from 9:51 to 19:27 is a sizable expansion of Mark 10:1-11:10, presenting events as Jesus journeyed to Jerusalem. Presuming Jesus was in the area of the Sea of Galilee for the events recorded earlier in Chapter 9, then it would be a journey of about seventy miles south to Jerusalem (verse 51).

The Samaritans were residents of the district of

Samaria, located south of Galilee between Galilee and Judea. The central town of the Samaritans was known as Samaria. In 1 Kings 16:24 we learn that Omri, a king of Israel, *bought the hill of Samaria,* and built upon it a city which he named Samaria (meaning *place of watch*) after the owner of the hill, Shemer, from whom he had bought it. It was the capitol of the Northern Kingdom known as Israel. For other references to the Samaritans in Luke, see 10:33 and 17:16.

Samaria had long had a negative image, going all the way back to the time of Ahab, who had erected there a pagan altar to Baal (1 Kings 16:32). Elisha made the city his headquarters (2 Kings 5:3-9; 6:32). The idolatry of the people, combined with worship of God, continued until after the fall of Jerusalem (2 Kings 17:25-41). Because of intermarriage with other nationalities, the Samaritans were not of pure Jewish blood. Josephus, the ancient Jewish historian, notes that when the Jews were in prosperity, the Samaritans claimed to be their blood-kin. Yet when the Jews were in adversity, the Samaritans claimed no relationship with them, and to be of Assyrian descent.

The Samaritans also created a rival place of worship to the Temple in Jerusalem on Mount Gerizim. Although their temple was destroyed in 128 B.C. by John Hyrcanus, worshipers continued to use the site as their place of worship up to and beyond the time of Jesus (see John 4:20-21).

For these reasons the Jews had no dealings with the Samaritans (John 4:9). Although the most direct route from Galilee to Jerusalem went through Samaria, most Jewish travelers avoided Samaria by traveling an indirect route. Thus it was not surprising for Jesus that the people would not receive him (verse 53) when they perceived that as a Jew he was heading to Jerusalem to worship in the Temple there at the feast of the Passover.

The resentment and prejudice of the disciples toward the Samaritans was evident in their interest in calling fire to *come down from heaven to destroy them* (NIV; NRSV = *and consume*). This was in the spirit of Elijah, the prophet, who twice called down fire from heaven upon the soldiers of Ahaziah, the idolatrous king, who had sent them to seize Elijah because of his condemnation of the king's idolatry (2 Kings 1:2-12). It was also rather presumptive of the disciples to think they had this prophetic power. Interestingly, Jesus' rebuke fell upon the disciples rather than the Samaritans (verse 55).

Priorities for Discipleship (9:57-62)

The observation of Jesus in verse 58 dealt with the cost and sacrifice one must be prepared to undertake to be a genuine disciple of Jesus.

The request in verse 59 was not simply for permission to arrange a funeral. Instead, it meant to delay a change in commitment until after fulfilling all obligations toward a parent as long as that parent lived. Then, after the death of the parent, discipleship would be undertaken. The response of Jesus (verse 60) was to the effect that past obligations must be surrendered to others to carry out while the follower pursued new obligations of discipleship. There were now new priorities. It is also possible to look at his injunction to be saying, "Let the spiritually dead bury their own dead." In other words, let those who have refused to follow Jesus take care of the others who have remained in darkness.

To say farewell to those at home (verse 61) may well have been a long-term process. It may have meant waiting until the death or the dissolution of home relationships. Jesus summed up the priorities in a figure of speech easily observed and understood by his hearers, for plowing was done by them and all around them. In plowing, the farmer had to keep his eyes on the direction he was going in order to keep the furrow straight. If he turned to look back while moving with the plow, the plow could well move into a crooked pattern and away

from the desired direction. To be *fit* means to be ready
for use.

Sending Out of Emissaries (10:1-24)

The ones sent out were to be heralds of the one coming
behind them (verse 1). Here again Jesus became a second
Moses in choosing seventy. Moses had done the same in
choosing assistants (elders) to help him in leading the
people while in the wilderness (Numbers 11:16-17,
24-25). This tradition had been carried on through the
creation of the Sanhedrin, the ruling body of the Jewish
religion, consisting of seventy members.

Note again the use of a farming reference (verse 2),
familiar to his hearers.

Compare verses 4-11 with the guidelines given by
Jesus to the Twelve in 9:1-5. They are similar in content,
with the guidelines to the seventy being an enlargement
of those given to the Twelve.

The traditional Jewish greeting, "Peace"(*Shalom*), was
to be used (verse 5) and be authentic. To remain in the
same house (verse 7) earning *wages* meant that they were
to be willing to work at worthwhile tasks and not to walk
off leaving tasks unfinished. They were to be dependable
and thorough.

Note the close relationship between healing and the
nearness of the Kingdom in verse 9. It suggests that in
the process of healing the kingdom of God is both
operational and apparent.

Regarding the *dust of your town* (verse 11), see the
commentary on 9:5.

Sodom (verse 12) was a town which, along with the
town of Gomorrah, was destroyed because of its
sinfulness (Genesis 19:24-28).

Chorazin (verse 13) was a city of Galilee near
Capernaum where Jesus preached, but the residents were
unresponsive. *Bethsaida* was described in the commentary
on 9:10. *Tyre and Sidon* (see also 6:17) were condemned by

the prophets for arrogance and idolatry (Isaiah 23; Ezekiel 26-28). *Capernaum,* the name meaning *exalted to heaven* (verse 15; see also 4:31; 7:1) was on a hillside. As Jesus left these areas, he said in essence that they had had exposure to spiritual truth. Having had that opportunity, their fate is far worse by their rejection or indifference than that of those who never had this new spiritual opportunity.

The imagery of Satan falling from heaven (verse 18) is found elsewhere in Scripture (see Isaiah 14:12; John 12:31; Revelation 12:9). It is an expression of victory over evil and the power of evil. The word *Satan* means *adversary* and is rooted in a Hebrew word meaning *obstruct.* The name was used for the devil, or chief of the devils, who was behind all evil.

To tread *upon snakes and scorpions* (verse 19) was to be victorious over that which was painful and life-threatening.

The real cause for rejoicing is not one's spiritual abilities to bring life to others but God's gracious acceptance of even us into life. The imagery of names being recorded in a divine book of life is a familiar scriptural figure of speech (see Exodus 32:32-33; Psalm 69:28; Daniel 12:1; Revelation 3:5).

Verses 21-24 again refer to the paradox that, while spiritual truth may be all around us, only a few see or know it, and they find it through divine revelation. This is also true of the messianic secret (verse 22; see commentary on 9:36) which is revealed to only a few.

What *many prophets and kings desired to see* (verse 24) was the messiah and the messianic age.

The Good Samaritan (10:25-37)

The *lawyer* (verse 25, NRSV; NIV = *an expert in the law*) was probably the same as a scribe, that is, a person who studied and interpreted the Jewish law. The Gentile readers would more readily understand the designation of lawyer.

The question asked is also later asked in Luke's account by a *ruler* in 18:18. In Mark's account of this incident the question is, *Which commandment is the first of all?* (Mark 12:28). Jesus was being "tested"by the inquirer as he sought to see whether Jesus would give the accepted and traditional response that such life was obtained through obedience to the law. However, Jesus turned the question back upon the inquirer (verse 26).

The quotations offered by the lawyer (verse 27) included the famous Shema (Deuteronomy 6:4-5), a central affirmation in Jewish faith. Additionally, he quoted a sentence from elsewhere in the law (Leviticus 19:18*b*) about attitude toward one's neighbor. Jesus did not initiate the idea of loving neighbor as self; it was part of the inherited law.

The lawyer sought to *justify* (verse 29) asking the first question by asking a second question, seeking clarification of a point as a means of following up the first question.

Jesus' reference to Jerusalem was appropriate in the light of his own journeying in that direction and his hearers' familiarity with that route from Jerusalem to Jericho (verse 30). It was a crooked trail descending over 3,000 feet from the green hills around Jerusalem to the desert wilderness below sea level at Jericho. About halfway down the present roadway are the ruins of a building dating back to Roman times called the Inn of the Good Samaritan. The winding road surrounded by many huge boulders and nearby caves made it a likely place of ambushes by robbers.

A *Levite* (verse 32) was similar to a lay leader in the congregation, assisting the priest in caring for altarware and other physical properties in the place of worship, providing musical leadership, ushering, and teaching. This person had made a commitment to a life of service to God. *Levite* comes from a Hebrew term meaning a person pledged for a debt or vow. Originally they were from the tribe of Levi (descendants of Levi, one of the sons of Jacob) and were charged with the care of the sanctuary. (See Numbers 1:50-53; 3:6-9, 25-37; 4:1-33.)

The central feature and surprise of this story is that a

Samaritan (verse 33) showed compassion for the Jewish victim when those of his own background and religious tradition would not. For the background of the Samaritans, see the commentary on 9:51-56.

He placed *oil and wine* on his body (verse 34) because of their use in that time as therapeutic ointments.

A denarius (verse 35) was a type of currency worth about one-fourth of a cent today, but with much more value in Jesus' time (see 7:41).

Visit with Martha and Mary (10:38-42)

Martha, Mary, and Lazarus were brother and sisters who lived in Bethany (or a nearby place) in southern Galilee. The word *Martha* means *lady* or *mistress. Mary* is a form of the Hebrew word *mirium.* In the Fourth Gospel, she is identified as the one who anoints Jesus with oil (John 12:3). They were probably among the devoted followers or disciples of Jesus in addition to the Twelve.

§ § § § § § §

The Message of Luke 9:51-10:42

In this section, beginning with the chosen route through Samaria and ending with the choices of Martha and Mary, Jesus is forcing persons to face the questions of priorities. To what are we committed? Then Jesus intends to give a new definition of the priority of loving God and neighbor. It requires seeing and identifying with the unloved in companionship and care. We are to become more sensitive to where human hurt and need exist and become a source of strength and part of the solution to them. We must avoid letting customs or busy-ness rob us of our awareness of this calling and these priorities. Our faith must bring an over-arching purpose to our living, a heart to our feeling, and caring hands and feet to our doing.

§ § § § § § §

LUKE 11:1–13:9

Introduction to These Chapters

As Jesus continued to journey toward Jerusalem, the teaching portion of his ministry took on ever larger dimensions in Luke's account. There were more sayings than events. Geographical surroundings took second place to instructional recollections. There was more that Jesus wanted his followers to know and understand. And this Luke recalls for us in the following format.

    I. Commentary on Prayer (11:1-13)
   II. On Evil Within (11:14-36)
  III. On Pharisees and Lawyers (11:37-12:3)
  IV. On the Worth of Persons (12:4-9)
   V. On the Potential of Words (12:10-12)
  VI. On the Place of Things (12:13-34)
 VII. Call to Obedient Watchfulness (12:35-48)
VIII. On Divisiveness of Discipleship (12:49-59)
  IX. Call for Repentance (13:1-9)

Commentary on Prayer (11:1-13)

Jesus' pattern of withdrawal to pray was repeated. The disciples had apparently seen prayer as a source of power and sustenance in Jesus' life and ministry. Thus they asked, *Lord, teach us to pray*. Rabbis usually taught prayers to their disciples. John the Baptist must have done the same.

The use of the term *Father* (verse 2) was not original with Jesus. Such references are found in the Old Testament. However, by using this term Jesus reaffirmed the personal nature of God. The "hallowing" of the name of God was an important custom of reverence in the Jewish religious tradition. The name of God (*Yahweh*) was considered so sacred that it was not even to be uttered. Instead, another word (*Adonai*) was substituted when speaking of God.

The essence of the petition for *bread* is for one day's supply of bread. Some interpret it to mean, "Give us this day the bread we need for tomorrow." In bread is found the basic physical elements essential to life. Also, bread has special spiritual symbolism through its use in worship and family rituals. So it can be seen as a prayer for the essentials for body and spirit.

This prayer includes and expresses the essential needs from Jesus' perspective. By including a petition for forgiveness (verse 4), Jesus identified forgiveness as a basic need within every person. One must have a forgiving spirit to be able to receive forgiveness. By using *indebted* Luke picks up the word Matthew used in reporting this petition (Matthew 6:9-13), but interprets that to mean *sins*.

Lead us not into temptation (NIV; NRSV = *do not bring us to the time of trial*) is another way of saying *deliver us from evil*, which may have been added to help clarify the intention of the petition. The combined petitions for forgiveness and divine direction seek to assist believers in dealing with the guilt of sin in the past and the threat of sin in the future.

The happenings reported in verses 5-8 suggest that even if friendship did not automatically elicit a response to meet one's need, surely persistence would obtain a response. It would not be uncommon for a traveler to arrive at night, for travel was often done at night to avoid the extreme heat of the day. The summary of the implications of the story in verses 9-10 makes it clear that it was told not to compare God with a reluctant friend, but to urge initiative and persistence in prayer.

Recall the reference to serpents and scorpions in 10:19 when the seventy were being sent out. Again, in verses 11-12, they stand for that which was painful and life-threatening.

The appraisal, *who are evil* (verse 13, NRSV; NIV-*though you are evil*), suggests that Jesus regarded all humanity as sinful and thus needing the forgiveness sought in the prayer he had just taught.

On Evil Within (11:14-36)

The comment just made on verse 13 forms an ideological backdrop for what is taught in these verses.

A demon that was mute (verse 14) means a demon seen as causing the inability to speak within this man. *Beelzebul* (verses 15, 18) was the name or title for the prince of devils or demons, the one who had power over evil. The word may have its origins in the name of the pagan god, Baal, or a god of Ekron with a similar name. When accused of casting out evil by the power of the evil one, Jesus turned the accusation back on his accusers. Since their religious leaders also practiced exorcism, they must have been doing it also by the power of evil if Jesus was doing such as they accused him.

The phrase *finger of God* (verse 20) is an Old Testament image (see Exodus 8:19; Deuteronomy 9:10). Here it is used to represent the power of God. If God's activity was taking place among them, the divine Kingdom was in their midst.

Verses 21-23 suggest that one's commitment must be very strong and unassailable with no weakness or hesitation or division through which evil could enter to conquer and destroy.

Spirits were always seeking a lodging place (verse 24). (Recall the event in 8:32-33 when the evil spirits, set free, entered the swine and destroyed them.) Waterless wastelands would be a temporary dwelling place. Verses

24-26 suggest that deliverance is not enough in the battle with evil. Deliverance must be accompanied by defense.

The exclamation in verse 27 praises the mother of Jesus in figures of speech commonly used then. Jesus sees a greater blessedness (or a blessed and happy state) for those in the future who are faithful to their new and genuine spiritual insight by acting upon it. This future blessedness for them would be greater than any past blessedness simply related to him.

The Old Testament prophet Jonah (verse 29) preached to the residents of Nineveh (Jonah 3) warning of destruction. So Jesus sought to do.

The Queen of the south (verse 31) was the Queen of Sheba in southern Arabia who traveled to Jerusalem to see the wealth of Solomon (1 Kings 10:1-13). Having witnessed the wisdom and glory of Solomon, she could testify by comparison to the greater wisdom and glory of Christ. The residents of Nineveh repented at the preaching of Jonah, but even more than repentance happened through the preaching of Jesus.

If the *eye* (verse 34) is diseased, or not *sound*, one's vision is reduced because full light is blocked by the defect. What the eye clearly discovers and receives spiritually will determine the light within in comparison with evil within (verses 34, 36).

On Pharisees and Lawyers (11:37-12:3)

For a discussion of the Pharisees (verse 37), see the commentary on 5:17 when they are first encountered in Luke. They are encountered again in 5:30; 6:2; 7:30, 36. This was Jesus' second meal with a Pharisee.

The tradition of washing before a meal (verse 38) was not required by the law but was practiced by the Pharisees as an additional expression of the desire for ceremonial cleanliness. This washing even had prescribed forms. *The cup and the dish* (verse 39) were used here by Jesus to stand for the washing of the body.

Verse 41 refers to dues or offerings that were expected or required to be paid to the Temple. Jesus was calling for giving that was representative of one's very self rather than what one handled.

The *tithe* (verse 42) was a *tenth* part of one's income, which was offered to God. In its original form, the Mosaic law called for a tithe on fruits of the ground and cattle, since they were like income (Leviticus 27:30-32). The Pharisees expanded the concept in interpreting the law to include even herbs as fruit of the ground, of which *mint* and *rue* were examples. They went very far to give these things, but nowhere to share the love of God in action and advocacy.

The best seats *in the synagogues* (verse 43) were those in front surrounding the Torah and facing the congregation. They were physically prominent, but those sitting in them may have been lacking in authentic spiritual prominence.

Verse 45 again may refer to the scribes who studied and interpreted or applied the Jewish law and the commentaries on the law (Mishnah). They would point out legal obligations but offer no assistance (verse 46).

Verses 47-48 suggest a continuing disregard, even silencing, for the genuine and demanding word of God as spoken by divine spokespersons.

Abel (verse 51) was the first person killed in the Old Testament narrative (Genesis 4:8). Zechariah was the last person killed in that narrative (2 Chronicles 24:20-22; Zechariah 1:1).

The lawyers (verse 52) knew the letter of the law but not its spirit, and thus kept others from finding that spirit.

In verse 53 the reactions are in response to what Jesus said to the Pharisees and lawyers or scribes.

Yeast is put into dough to make it rise. The Pharisaic stress upon legal obedience, but with blindness to commitment of personhood to genuine devotion to God and one another, can "cover up" one's spiritual hollowness, which ultimately will be seen for what it really is.

On the Worth of Persons (12:4-9)

The Greek word translated *hell* (verse 5) was *Gehenna*. This is the only use of this word in Luke's account. *Gehenna* means *valley of Hinnom,* which was located just west and south of Jerusalem. Its narrow confines served as the depository for garbage from the city, where it was burned with unceasing fires. In the Old Testament there was a pagan cult that worshiped Molech by making their children go through fires in this valley (2 Kings 23:10). Josiah had destroyed pagan altars there and had polluted the place by taking bones from the tombs and dumping them there (2 Kings 23:14).

The Jewish faith did not have an expansive concept of life after death. At death the soul went to Sheol, a place of the dead, to await reunion with the body at the time of resurrection. In the New Testament the Greek word *haides,* or Hades (meaning *unseen*) was used for Sheol. This was seen as a dark place of shadows, where there might be punishments or rewards.

Hell, or Gehenna, was beyond Sheol. From Sheol one's soul might escape, but Hell was a place of ultimate destruction by fire of both soul and body.

The warning is against those forms or persons of evil who can destroy from both within and without.

Sparrows (verse 6) were among the cheapest items sold.

That *the hairs of your head are all numbered* (verse 7) was a way of expressing the worth of every person. The apostle Paul recalls this figure of speech in offering hope to his fellow sailors in the storm at sea (Acts 27:34).

The Greek word for *acknowledges* (verse 8) can be translated *agrees with* or *confesses.* The Son of man here is identified as serving in the role of an advocate before God, or the emissaries (*angels*) of God.

On the Potential of Words (12:10-12)

Here Jesus differentiated between words against himself and words against the Holy Spirit (verse 10). The Greek word translated *blasphemes* means to speak lightly or profanely of sacred things. Blasphemy was regarded so seriously that under the Mosaic Law one who blasphemed was stoned to death (Leviticus 24:16).

The work of the Holy Spirit was to unveil God and God's purposes and presence. If one continuously took lightly or indifferently what the Spirit was saying, then one would be, in effect, persistently resisting God. One could not be "forgiven" because one would never be seeking God or receiving the message of forgiveness if there was total disregard to the Spirit.

The contrast is portrayed between one who listens to the Spirit and one who does not listen. One who does not listen loses even the possibility of forgiveness. One who does listen will find the resources to rise above confrontation and fear. *The Holy Spirit will teach you at that very hour what you ought to say* (verse 12). The teaching role of the Holy Spirit is identified.

On the Place of Things (12:13-34)

In this set of teachings Jesus again used word-pictures taken from the daily experiences and observations of his hearers: land, barns, treasure, ravens, lilies, spinning, grass, purses, and so forth.

Underlying all the Bible's teachings is the theme of the tendency of persons to center their lives on themselves. In the biblical view a current within and around us pushes us toward self-centeredness. Furthermore, as a result of surrendering to this current, we move on through self-centeredness to self-seeking. We feel that if we can just get all we can for ourselves, all our problems will be solved. Thus there came the person to Jesus seeking *the inheritance* from his brother (verse 13). Jesus' parable gives another illustration of this drifting tendency through self-centeredness to self-seeking.

Underlying this set of teachings is the spiritual principle that our calling as servants of God and followers of Jesus is to seek God's purposes for one another and share necessities with one another. As we pursue that goal, God will provide what we need (verses 31-32).

A *cubit* (verse 25, NRSV; see NIV footnote) was twenty inches. The material *glory* of Solomon (verse 27) is described in 1 Kings 9:26-10:25.

The idea of *purses that do not wear out* means purses whose material contents have been given away (*sell your possessions and give alms*, verse 33), to be replaced with heavenly, or divinely bestowed, eternal treasures.

Call to Obedient Watchfulness (12:35-48)

Lest one presume that by virtue of the promise made in verse 32 all was assured for the follower of Jesus and no response on that person's part was needed, Jesus summoned his disciples to a high degree of watchfulness and guardedness.

Being *dressed* for action (verse 35) refers to the long flowing outer garment worn in Palestine. In work situations, of necessity the lower portion was folded up into the waistband or belt to give freedom of movement. This was what was meant by *girding up* one's *loins*.

The *wedding banquet* (verse 36) may or may not have been for the marriage of the master. It simply refers to a social event which would continue, as marriage feasts did, until very late at night. Thus the servants might well have gone to sleep because of the lateness of the hour, but the few who were awake and watching would be rewarded for their alertness (verse 37). The night was divided by Roman custom into four watches: 6:00 to 10:00 P.M., 10:00 P.M. to 2:00 A.M., 2:00 to 6:00 A.M., and 6:00 to 10:00 A.M. The *second watch* (verse 38, NIV; NRSV =

middle of the night) would be from 10:00 P.M. to 2:00 A.M., and the third from 2:00 to 6:00 A.M.

The idea of watchfulness and preparedness will be a strong motif in all the New Testament. In large measure it grows out of the concept expressed in verse 40. For illustrations read 1 Thessalonians 5:2; 2 Peter 3:10; Revelation 19:9. The reference to the Son of man *coming* was interpreted by the early church to mean a future or second coming known by the Greek word *parousia*.

The sensitivities unveiled in the parables in verses 36-38 and 39-40 are expanded upon in an additional parable in verses 42-48. The repetition of parables on this theme indicates the importance of the concept of responsible watchfulness to Jesus and by Jesus for his followers. This third parable describes the extreme of irresponsibility by the *servant* (NIV; NRSV = *slave*) when that servant loses a sense of watchfulness. One thing leads to another: abuse of others, self-indulgence, drunkenness (verse 45).

A Divisiveness of Discipleship (12:49-59)

The background of the statements by Jesus in verses 49-50 was possibly the statements by John the Baptist in 3:16-17 where he spoke both of *baptism* and *fire* to come from the one coming after him. *Fire* was used as a figure of speech for judgment. The *fire* was to be *cast* by Jesus but the baptism was to be received by Jesus. Since he had already received baptism by water, some other type of baptism was expected. This baptism for Jesus may have been the baptism of suffering and death. Thus Jesus would have been saying that he would both bring and also receive judgment and trial.

By virtue of this cost to disciples and Jesus, some would continue to follow and some would fall away. Family members would be divided among themselves as to allegiance to Christ (verses 52-53). (Remember Jesus' comments about his own mother and brother, 8:19-21.)

A *cloud* brought the possibility of rain to an arid climate and was a source of hope (verse 54). A *south wind blowing* (verse 55) from more temperate zones brought the prospect of dry heat and dust, and would be a threat to be feared. So these were obvious signs of weather to come. *Hypocrites* were blinded by their own self-righteousness. They could not read the spiritual signs around them through the ministry of Jesus, which would tell them of what God had in store (verse 56).

Verses 57-59 warn that in spite of the divisiveness Jesus caused, there should constantly be attempts at reconciliation lest diviseness rob his hearers of their worth and potential at the day of judgment.

A *penny* (verse 59) was the smallest coin in value in circulation.

Call for Repentance (13:1-9)

The exact incident referred to in verse 13 is unknown. Josephus, the ancient Jewish historian, does mention hostile acts toward the Jews during Pilate's reign. It may be that Pilate had carried out some act of aggression while sacrifices were being offered, resulting in blood being shed by Galileans (who would have been from Jesus' home area) at the altar of sacrifice.

Pontius Pilate was first mentioned by Luke in 3:1. He was the Roman governmental representative, or procurator, in Judea, serving from A.D. 26–36. He was immensely disliked by the Jews because he had permitted his troops to carry ensigns with images of the emperor on them into Jerusalem. He also sought to use Temple money to construct a water viaduct.

Jesus' hearers are called upon to *repent* (verse 3) in the light of all the signs around them.

The incident referred to in verse 4 is also not known. *The tower* would have been part of the defenses of Jerusalem near the pool of Siloam. Destruction falling upon some does not indicate that they were worse sinners than others who escaped injury. All are subject to God's judgment.

The vineyard story (13:6-9) concludes this section by

suggesting that imminent judgment and destruction upon the faithless is at hand. The only thing delaying it is God's willingness to provide one more opportunity for faithfulness to come forth.

§ § § § § § §

The Message of Luke 11:1–13:9

As Jesus moves toward Jerusalem and continues his teachings, he invites his followers to utilize prayer as a means of self-awareness and awareness of God's purposes. He pushes his hearers toward authentic lives and genuine spirituality.

Much of what is taught in this section suggests two attitudes that could combat the drift toward spiritual blindness or insensitivity and also shape the priorities for our future lifestyle. One was to weigh carefully values that last against values of the moment. We are to more responsibly weigh moments, words, things, persons, attitudes. Jesus called upon his hearers to raise the question in everything they did and sought as to whether it was something of lasting value—and to be watchful in pursuit of eternal values.

Also, Jesus affirmed that every movement is important. He called upon his disciples to live life aware of the limits of time and opportunity. Their daily choices and achievements were to be governed by the sense that every moment was important and should be used in the best way for the service and purpose of God. The idea is summed up in the word *Watch!* which would be picked up elsewhere in the New Testament. His followers are to be watchful—of time, choices, purposes—in faith. This is not to be watching and waiting but watching and doing.

§ § § § § § §

LUKE 13:10–16:31

Introduction to These Chapters

The journey to Jerusalem continued, as did the
teachings of Jesus en route. This section of teachings
covers a number of different topics, largely unrelated to
each other. These particular teachings were most often
stimulated by events or encounters. Thus it is a blending
of actions and attitudes, divided as follows:

Confrontation over the Sabbath (13:10-17)

Note that Jesus was still following the practice of being
in the local synagogue (verse 10) on the sabbath day.

The woman's disease appears to have been a form of
arthritis. From the biblical viewpoint, it was seen to be
caused by a destructive spirit, as were most illnesses,
especially those of a chronic nature.

All work was forbidden on the sabbath (Exodus
20:9-10) and healing was considered to be work (verse
14). Jesus used the comparison with the common practice
of releasing farm animals on the sabbath and leading
them to obtain refreshment they needed for their bodies.
If the welfare of an animal was important enough to

warrant disregard of sabbath restrictions, then restoring the health of a person's body should be all the more justifiable on the sabbath (verse 16).

The Nature of the Kingdom (13:18-30)

In Palestine the mustard was not a simple garden plant, but grew to such size that it could be referred to as a *tree* (verse 19). It grew as high as eight to twelve feet. Thus birds could nest *in its branches.* The seed, however, was as small as any other plant seed. A little created a lot. It became a shelter and a home.

Yeast (verse 21) meant any substance that produced fermentation in dough and thus caused the rising of bread. Usually, leaven was a portion of old dough in a highly fermented state. The leaven was not apparent after the dough had risen and thus it was hid from view. *Three measures* was a very *large amount* of meal or flour, more than a bushel. Again a little dynamic substance changed the nature of a large amount surrounding it.

Jesus continued *to Jerusalem* (verse 22). This comment by Luke may be for dramatic effect as well as being a descriptive reminder.

The entrance to most Palestinian homes was small and *narrow* (verse 24). Only one person could enter at a time. Being small, it was more easily covered or blocked by the residents of the house for protection or privacy. The conversation recorded in verses 25-27 took place through the closed door, so the *owner of the house* could not see those knocking on the outside.

Weeping and gnashing of teeth (verse 28) was a familiar figure of speech in Jewish literature for despair and frustration. *Gnash* could also be translated *grind.* The frustration is over the fact that one can be close to the Kingdom and the Kingdom's heroes, and even presume one's right to enter, but miss out on it, to one's dismay. Simultaneously, unknown persons from a distance (probably the Gentiles and even persons of other nationalities) may be eligible by insight and spirit to be a part of the Kingdom (that is, sit at table *in the kingdom of God,* verse 29). For many Jews the thought that non-Jews could have intimate fellowship with the spiritual heroes of their faith while they themselves were excluded would be immensely disturbing. To invite someone to one's table was a custom and expression of gracious hospitality and mutual respect. So the list of residents of the kingdom of God will be full of surprise listings (verse 30) by God's gracious invitation.

A Warning and a Lament (13:31-35)

For commentary on the *Pharisees* (verse 31) see the remarks on 5:17. Here we find Pharisees befriending Jesus. Although Jesus had spoken himself about dangerous events awaiting him (9:22), this was the first time in Luke's account that someone had warned Jesus of danger. This helps us to remember that within any given group, all are not the same types of persons. Nicodemus, who assisted in burying the body of Jesus (John 19:39), was a Pharisee, and Joseph of Arimathea, in whose tomb Jesus was buried, may have been a Pharisee.

Herod (verse 31) was the ruler of Galilee (see 23:6-7). Thus this incident must have been misplaced in the narrative and belongs in one of the Galilean narratives. Remember that Herod had already heard of Jesus and been curious about him (9:7-9). Although a *fox* (verse 32) is known for dangerous cunning, some commentators point out that this word is more often used in rabbinical literature as a word of contempt suggesting an unimportant individual.

At first Jesus appeared to defy Herod in his response, suggesting he would continue his ministry there despite this threat (verse 32). Yet by now Jesus appeared to be under a compulsion or obsession not only to get to Jerusalem but even to die there, if he must die (verse 33). There was a blending of compassion with hurt as Jesus lamented over Jerusalem (verse 34). By using the word *prophets* here, he was probably not speaking specifically of an Old Testament prophet but in general about persons who were faithful spokespersons for God.

Verse 35 portrays a contrast between the forsaken or desolate spiritual state of Jerusalem and the fact that into the very midst of this state would enter one who authentically *comes in the name of the Lord.* This is a paradox. Into the midst of the least deserving will come the one God has promised and sent.

Teachings at a Pharisee's House (14:1-24)

Note again that a Pharisee showed hospitality to Jesus (verse 1, see 7:36). Again Luke wants us to see that all Pharisees were not alike.

Dropsy (verse 2) was a term used to describe the condition of undue fluid collection in tissues or cavities of the body, usually caused by heart or kidney disease.

In Luke's account there were four occasions when Jesus exercised a healing ministry on the sabbath (see also 4:38; 6:6; 13:13). John's account has two additional incidents (John 5:9; 9:14) and Mark's account has one additional incident (Mark 1:21-26).

In the last account in Luke of a healing on the sabbath resulting in criticism of Jesus, after Jesus offered his defense *his adversaries were put to shame* (13:17, NRSV; NIV = *humiliated*). This may explain why on this occasion his critics *were silent* (verse 4). As he had on the previous occasion, again he responded by showing how the essential needs of animals were met on the sabbath (verse 5). The implication was that in the light of this sabbath practice, surely meeting the essential needs of persons was justified.

Apparently, this dinner occasion was marked by a considerable degree of formality with the places next to the guest and host being *the places of honor* (verse 7). These were the most desired seats.

The *wedding feast* (verse 8) was one of the most celebrative of all social occasions and also an occasion that most of his hearers had attended and would attend. Nothing would be more embarrassing than to sit in one of the places of honor and then find that you had sat in the wrong seat and have to move. The obvious lesson is stated in verse 11.

In the midst of this formalized occasion, Jesus cautioned his host not to fall into the trap of offering hospitality and friendship only to those who could return the same. True *blessedness* (verse 14) or happiness was found in offering these to persons who seldom received them and could not return them. Repayment would be in the form of tributes these persons might offer when resurrected among the *just* or righteous in God's sight, for some of these unlikely persons would be there (13:29-30). Such an openness toward those invited would be like that of God's invitation (see 13:28-30).

The exclamation in verse 15, *Blessed is he who shall eat bread in the kingdom of God,* came from someone who sensed that Jesus was really talking about a togetherness in spiritual sustenance to be experienced in the kingdom of God as Jesus spoke to his host about banquet invitations. At least the comments of Jesus made the hearer think of the kingdom of God. This led Jesus to offer a parable that did relate to the Kingdom (verse 16). This was an expansion of his admonitions to the Pharisee (verses 12-14). Now Jesus became more emphatic in pointing out that those close to Kingdom possibilities for their lives missed out because of poor priority choices (verses 17-20). And those never expecting anything good became the recipients of the Kingdom's gifts and sustenance (verses 21-24).

The Cost of Authentic Discipleship (14:25-35)

The popularity of Jesus remained intact, perhaps even more so after the sensitivities to the poor and disabled just expressed. Yet Jesus, en route to Jerusalem, was aware of the demands and cost of genuine discipleship. He had begun to point this out in earlier dialogue with the disciples (9:22-24) before journeying toward Jerusalem. He had expanded upon it in warnings such as 9:62. Now to the multitudes Jesus stressed that following him would be at a cost. What was stated to the *large crowds* (verse 25) in verses 26-27 was a repeat of that previously stated to the Twelve (9:23; 12:52-53; see the commentaries on those passages).

The *tower* was probably a guard tower for a vineyard to guard against theft or animals. The parables of the tower builder (verses 28-30) and the king at war (verses 31-32) both stress the need to accurately calculate the cost before undertaking a demanding project. By telling the two stories Jesus pointed out that the same need applies to the ordinary person and to those in exalted positions, the high and the low (verse 33). To *give up* all that he has (verse 33) is a call both to sacrifice and to reprioritize one's life. *Salt* was extremely important in that time and place as a preservative. If its sodium content was lost, it had no value, for it could not fulfill its purpose, either for crops or for *manure*. So if one loses that which is the essence or heart of discipleship (such as a willingness to sacrifice and a priority of purpose), that type of allegiance to Christ is worthless.

Attitude Toward the Lost (15:1-32)

Tax collectors (verse 1), because of their corruption and exploitation of persons, are specified among the *sinners*. Yet they were attracted to Jesus. The accusation of *the Pharisees and scribes* (NRSV; NIV = *teachers of the law*) had been leveled at Jesus earlier when he ate at the home of Levi, the tax collector (5:29-30).

The three famous parables that follow, the lost sheep (verse 3-7), the lost coin (verses 8-10), and the lost sons (verses 11-24), all have certain characteristics in common.

They all describe happenings well-known to his hearers and experienced, in one form or another, by all of them. They all emphasize the persistent concern and openness of the one who has lost something to have it back. They all end on the note of joy when that takes place. The fact that Jesus used three stories to deal with one theme emphasizes its importance to Jesus and his strong desire to communicate this message clearly to everyone.

The shepherds were nomads, moving from place to place to find something growing for the sheep to feed upon in the midst of areas of sparse vegetation (verse 4). Thus it would not be uncommon for a sheep to wander off or be left behind. It was rocky and uneven land. There were crevices and cliffs where a sheep might easily fall. Only when a count was made, perhaps at dusk, would the loss be discovered. If the lamb or sheep had fallen into a crevice or over a ledge, it would be necessary for the shepherd to lay it *on his shoulders* to carry it out to a place where it could walk.

The *silver coins* (verse 8) were called *drachmas*, a Greek coin similar in value to the Roman denarius. Although worth only about sixteen cents now, in that time it would have been a sizable amount in purchasing power. It could well have been most of the savings of this woman. Because she was a poor person, every coin counted. In telling these two stories Jesus communicated the message of a seeking God and joy over repentance to both men and women. They testify additionally to the sensitivity Jesus had for women.

The third parable is not just the story of the Prodigal Son, as it is so often called. It is the parable of *two sons* (verse 11), as is clearly stated at the outset. Both sons were lost, one lost in self-indulgence (verses 12-14) and one in self-centeredness and pride (verses 28-30).

Under the Mosaic law the father, at a time of his choice, would determine and announce a division of his possessions (Deuteronomy 21:15-17). The actual bestowal of these possessions would usually take place at death, but might take place during the father's lifetime. This younger son wanted his portion while his father was still living, and the father granted this wish (verse 12).

Wild living (verse 13, NIV; NRSV = *dissolute living*) can be translated *reckless* or *wasteful* living. It is from this verse that the designation *prodigal son* arises. A prodigal is primarily not a lost person, but a wasteful person.

Under the law, swine meat was not allowed in the Jewish diet (see Leviticus 11:26). The Talmud, or commentary upon the Jewish law, said, *Cursed is the man who tends swine.* Thus to *feed pigs* (verse 15) would be shameful and degrading for a Jew. This indicates how desperate this lad had become. Also it may indicate how insensitive he had become to his own religious tradition and upbringing. The *pods* (verse 16) may have come from the carob tree.

The key phrase in marking the transition in the direction of the story, and the son's life, is *when he came to himself* (verse 17, NRSV; NIV = *to his senses*). When he got in genuine touch on the inside with who he was and where he had descended, he changed the outside of his life. He feared and felt that his father justifiably might not accept him back as a son. So he prepared a statement in advance of the encounter with his father in which he would seek for only the status of a hired servant (verses 18-19), which was all he felt he deserved.

An embrace and a kiss were customary expressions of warm hospitality toward welcome guests. The father, however, had not waited at the house to bestow these. He had gone out on his own initiative to bestow them before the son's arrival (verse 20). The father interrupted the boy's well-prepared statement (verses 21-22), never allowing him to complete it. The *best robe* would have been one of exquisite craft and quality reserved for very important guests. The *ring* was a symbol of family status, perhaps a signet ring. The *sandals* marked him as a son, rather than a servant or slave. In passing it should be noted that the son was received in this manner even though he had wasted all that the father had given him, which could have been one-third of the father's possessions. Thus the father had had a sizable personal loss through the son's irresponsibility.

While the younger son was lost in his vice, the *elder son* (verse 25) was lost in his virtue (verse 28). He complained that in contrast to a *fatted calf* being killed for the banquet honoring his brother's return, not even a baby goat (*kid,* verse 29) had ever been killed for a meal in his behalf.

Until the father designated otherwise, all he possessed would go to the first-born son, who shared the supervision of it. Thus the father said, *You are always with me, and all that is mine is yours* (verse 31, NRSV).

All three parables end on the note of rejoicing over that which *was lost and is found* (verse 32), including the children of God.

Attitude Toward Possessions (16:1-31)

The *manager* (verse 1) could be compared to a junior executive, manager, or foreman today. Certain persons reported to him and he reported to his superior. The steward was praised *because he had acted shrewdly* (verse 8). It is possible that the debtors were persons from whom it was doubted that anything would be received because of their circumstances. The *rich man* had expected to have to write off their obligations as bad debts. But the steward, by initiative and compromise, born out a desperate fear of the account being required of him by the *rich man,* had achieved a high degree of return from the debtors (verses 5-7). In spite of his prudence, however, Jesus spoke of him as *dishonest* (verse 8).

Mammon (verses 9, 11, 13, NIV = *worldly wealth*; NRSV = *dishonest*) is an Aramaic word meaning wealth, money, property, and/or profit. Jesus alone uses it in the Bible and in a negative perspective.

The three earlier parables are clear in their meaning and the virtue of their central characters. This one is a contrast, puzzling and more difficult to interpret.

This parable seems to point a finger at the servants of God, who are not as wise and faithful in their spiritual tasks and opportunities as the secular are in their *dishonest* dealings. In verse 9 Jesus suggests that friendship with the unrighteous should be maintained until they see the futility and peril of their ways and look to the disciples of Jesus for eternal values and ways. Verses 10-12 are expansions of themes taken from this parable, leading off with comments on faithfulness and dishonesty.

The ultimate issue is expressed in verse 13. It is a summons to a choice between *God and mammon.* Once again Jesus calls for a clarification of priorities in life.

The ambivalent attitude of Luke toward the Pharisees shows in his appraisal that they *were lovers of money* (verse 14). He shows them in both positive and negative images. Jesus drew a distinction (verse 15) between the self-justification practiced by many Pharisees and God-justification which is an essential in the Kingdom (that is, the distinction between how we look in our own eyes and how we look in God's eyes).

As a sequel to the *law and the prophets* (verse 16), the *good news* (Greek *evangelion*) of the Kingdom had been proclaimed. So exciting and attractive was this news as Jesus had proclaimed it that persons even wanted to force their way into it. The Greek word translated *violently* describes a sense of urgent desire and desperate need. It is like a crowd of persons who have found something so very rare and desirable and even essential that they push and shove to get to it, to have it for themselves.

Jesus' comment on the law showed his respect for this

revelation of God within the tradition and his sense of being an interpreter of the spiritual essence of the law.

The teaching on divorce (verse 18) seems out of place here in the context of teachings about property and possessions. However, the status of women in that time was little more than property. A man could obtain divorce by simply renouncing his wife in a public statement before certain witnesses. By teaching that to divorce and then marry another person resulted in the commitment of adultery, Jesus was pointing out the worth of women and the sanctity of the marriage relationship. Wives could not be regarded as property nor the marriage relationship viewed as owner and owned. There were values in each person and in the covenantal relationship between the two to be regarded with respect.

Purple (verse 19) was a symbol of royalty or royal estate. The outer robe was purple and the undergarments made of linen. *Lazarus* means *one whom God helps*. This is the only place Luke uses this name. This may be an imaginary person in this story, and is not the person named Lazarus of Bethany raised from the dead in John's account. *What fell from the table* (verse 21) would be thrown outside as refuse. *Dogs* were regarded as unclean animals. Their attention to Lazarus would add to his shame.

Angels (verse 22) were seen as those who had the responsibility of transporting the spirits of the dead to the proper place. *Abraham's bosom* (NIV-*side*; NRSV-*to be with Abraham*) means a relationship of intimate closeness, usually reserved for a child. *Hades* was the word for Sheol (see the commentary on 12:5). The *great chasm* (verse 26) was seen as between the dwelling place of God with special servants who by spiritual faithfulness and unusual merit had gone to be with God, and the place of the dead who awaited the resurrection in Sheol.

Moses and the prophets are here interpreted as bearers of spiritual truth (verses 29, 31) who were not heard or understood by many persons. Even the witness of a resurrected one will not overcome the barriers within (such as indifference and self-contentment) to discover and respond to the truth. The real problem is not lack of truth offered but lack of receptivity within.

§ § § § § § §

The Message of Luke 13:10–16:31

There is a sense in which the plight of the two sons in the Parable of the Lost Sons (15:25-30) sums up the human weaknesses that Jesus addressed in the varied experiences and teachings of this section. The younger son was lost in human relationships—fleeing from a meaningful relationship with his father rather than seeking it, until need prompted him. He was lost in pursuit of possessions and then lost with the loss of possessions. He was lost in self-control, becoming more driven by impulses than committed to priorities. He was lost in values, giving himself to what seemed attractive. The end justified the means. He lost any high purpose or commitment in life. He lost his spiritual values and code for living.

The elder son was lost in spiritual pride and contentment. He was lost in a lack of compassion or a place for repentance.

To these circumstances all the portions of this section are addressed: the lostness in spiritual traditions that do not allow for healing, in relationships that are not inclusive, in shallow commitments that will not pay a price, in being possessed by possessions, in allowing no place for repentance in others nor seeing the need for it in ourselves. However, the greatest gladness God knows as our heavenly parent is when one of us, children of divine creation, having been *dead* becomes *alive* and who *was lost and is found* (15:32).

§ § § § § § §

LUKE 17:1–18:30

Introduction to These Chapters

This section is similar to the two preceding sections in format. It contains additional teachings of Jesus as he continued en route to Jerusalem. The primary focus of Luke continues to be more on what Jesus said than what he did. This focus narrows slightly as Jesus gave more specific directions to his disciples and also unveiled more central principles of the Kingdom.

Luke has organized the material as follows:
   I. Directions to Disciples (17:1-10)
  II. Encounter with the Ungrateful (17:11-19)
 III. Suddenness of the Kingdom's Coming (17:20-37)
  IV. Parables on Persistence and Prayer (18:1-14)
   V. Centrality of Children (18:15-17)
  VI. Self-denial Essential to Discipleship (18:18-30)

Directions to Disciples (17:1-10)

The Greek translated temptations *to sin* (verse 1, NIV) could more accurately be translated *stumbling blocks* or *causes of stumbling* (NRSV). It refers to that which, like underbrush or a vine, can snare you in your walking and trip you.

A *millstone* (verse 2) was a large round stone that lay on its flat side on a base. Between the stone and the base grain was placed to be ground, as the stone was turned around. This turning was usually done by attaching poles to an animal that walked around in a circle pulling the stone. An animal was used because the stone was so large and heavy.

The word sometimes translated *to sin* in verse 2 is again a word meaning *to stumble.*

Verses 3-4 contain Luke's form of the famous statement by Jesus in Matthew 18:21-22, calling for forgiveness to be offered not just seven times but up to *seventy times seven.*

Jesus used a *mustard seed* (verse 6) earlier as a figure of speech for teaching (see 13:19). Using it again, he stressed that a little faith could go a long way in bringing about Kingdom possibilities around us. The request of the disciples for increased faith may have been out of a desire to elevate their status by impressing others through their faith. Thus Jesus was led to offer the parable beginning in verse 7 as a corrective to them. An increase in faith would not bring spiritual pre-eminence, but only the ability to do what his hearers were supposed to do for the Kingdom in the first place. *We are unworthy servants* (verse 10, NIV; NRSV = *worthless slaves*) not just because we have only done what we were supposed to do, but also because God works through us as our faith enables God to so do.

Encounter with the Ungrateful (17:11-19)

When Jesus began his journey toward Jerusalem, he had passed through Samaria (9:51-56). Ordinarily, the route would not bring him back to Samaria, since Jerusalem was south of Samaria. Thus Jesus would have had to backtrack into Samaria for this event to have taken place at this time, or the episode may have been recorded out of its proper chronological order.

For background on Samaria and the strained relationship of Jews with Samaritans, read the commentary on 9:51-56 and 10:30-37, when Jesus visited Samaria and told a story about a Samaritan. For information on leprosy see the commentary on 5:12, when Jesus first encountered a leper in Luke's account.

Since lepers were banned from the community, they

often would reside together in an isolated settlement or even a cave. So it would not be uncommon to encounter *ten lepers* (verse 12). They *stood at a distance* because they were not allowed to mingle with other persons. They were so accustomed to rejection and scorn that their petition was first for *mercy* (verse 13, NRSV; NIV = *pity*) rather than healing.

The Mosaic law (Leviticus 13-14) regarding leprosy was very extensive and required the priest to go out and examine anyone thought to have been healed of the disease. If the priest was convinced that the disease was healed, then he was to carry out a ritual of cleansing as defined in Leviticus 14:1-9, involving sprinkling the victim with the blood of a bird and pronouncing the person clean. The person healed was to engage in acts of cleansing the body and offer prescribed sacrifices. Thus Jesus instructed those healed of leprosy to *go and show yourselves to the priests* (verse 14).

Apparently the leper colony was made up of both Jews and Samaritans. A common illness and community rejection had brought together those who ordinarily would have had nothing to do with each other. The natural impulse by any who were healed of this horrible illness, after being pronounced clean by the priest, would be immediately to hurry home and share the thrilling news with family members. Yet this one leper (verse 15) returned to Jesus. That he took the time to return is striking; but that, as a Samaritan, he took the time and effort to thank the Jewish teacher is inspiring. The *faith* of the Samaritan (verse 19) was not only a belief in what God could do but an expression in action of what he could do to express gratitude and overcome prejudice.

Suddenness of the Kingdom's Coming (17:20-37)

The Day of the Lord was the expression frequently used in the Old Testament for the coming of God's rule and day of God's reign. As this hope became more expressed in the prophetic utterances, events or signs were enumerated that would take place in advance of the Day of the Lord and be evidences of its coming. These are especially evident in Daniel (see Daniel 7) and the Jewish apocalyptic writers who wrote in the period between the two Testaments. However, in this passage (verses 20-21) Jesus indicated that there would be no signs of the Kingdom to come because, in him, the Kingdom was already in their midst.

However, as Jesus dealt with the subject of the coming of the kingdom of God, in Luke's account he spoke of it from a double perspective; having come and yet to come. The sayings of Jesus that follow in verses 22-35 speak of the *day of the Son of man* (verse 22) as though it is distinct from the coming of the Kingdom and is something yet to take place. One way of reconciling the two concepts is, first of all, to see that in the coming of Christ God has brought the Kingdom into the midst of humanity. From Christ we learn the nature of the Kingdom. In Christ we see the Kingdom modeled. Through Christ, and commitment to him, we find an entranceway into the Kingdom experience and understanding. Yet also Jesus as Son of man and Son of God is both present and yet to come, just as evidences of the kingdom of God are all around us, but the full expressions of the Kingdom are yet to be realized.

In verses 24-25 Jesus speaks of a role he is to play beyond the times of his suffering and rejection. This role of his invasion anew into humanity's life may be sudden and surprising (like *lightning,* verse 24; like the *flood,* verse 27; like the showering of *fire and sulphur,* verse 29), although ample prediction of it has been given.

The description of the *days of Noah* recalls the story of Noah's preparation of an ark of divine direction (Genesis 6:9-7:23). Those of his family who heeded God's warning and who went with him into the ark were saved from the flood waters. Undoubtedly, however, there were those who paid no heed to God's warnings or Noah's pleas. They went on with life as usual (verse 27) until it was too late. God acted as predicted.

Similarly, both Abraham and Lot were warned of an

act of judgment by God in the form of destruction to come upon the area where Lot and his family resided, Sodom and Gomorrah (Genesis 18:17-19:26). Again, there were those who paid no attention to God's warnings or Lot's pleas, going on with life as usual (verse 28) until it was too late. God acted as predicted. In spite of divine instructions not to look back at the destruction of Sodom, Lot's wife looked back and was turned into a *pillar of salt*. In stopping to witness the destruction, she may have been covered with the volcanic and sulfurous ash. So Jesus said, *Remember Lot's wife* (verse 32).

The *housetop* would have been the patio or high place from which one might see destruction at hand or the divine invasion taking place (verse 31).

Different people will be affected in different ways by God's sudden action (verses 33-35). Those who have surrendered their lives to God's purposes will find life continuing. Those who have sought to preserve life for their own selfish purposes will lose what little life they found (verse 33). Where *the vultures* (verse 37) gather as scavengers, what is left of the self-seeking will be found.

Parables on Persistence and Prayer (18:1-14)

The description of the judge as one *who neither feared God nor cared about men* (verse 2, NIV; NRSV = *nor had respect for people*) identifies him as one of independent judgment who was not swayed by pressure or tradition. A *widow* (verse 3) was one who was the object of special sensitivity and empathy in the Jewish tradition. The Mosaic law placed upon the community special obligations for the care and protection of widows.

The story does not compare God and the judge. Instead, it is intended to call for perseverance in prayer, as is indicated in the introductory statement about the parable in verse 1 (*should always pray*).

The *chosen* of God (verse 7) are those who have elected to be servants indeed of the divine will and purposes as revealed through Jesus.

The parable of the Pharisee and the tax collector (called

a *publican* in some earlier translations) (verses 9-14) appears only in Luke's account. It is a beautiful story of insight into prayer and the perspectives of Jesus. The Pharisee's prayer was *about* (NIV; NRSV = *by*) *himself*, as Jesus saw it. He was convincing himself more than God of his righteousness. Fasting was only required under the law on the Day of Atonement, and it was called *the fast* (see Acts 27:9). Additional fasting was for special merit and might even be done twice weekly (verse 12). Tithes were to be given of all one's produce (Numbers 18:26; Deuteronomy 14:22). However, this Pharisee tithed out of everything he received. (See the commentary on 11:42 for additional data on the Pharisees' practice of tithing.)

When the tax collector *beat his breast* (verse 13), he was engaging in an Eastern custom for expressing the deepest sorrow. To be *justified* (verse 14) meant to be right in the eyes of God.

Centrality of Children (18:15-17)

Still multitudes followed Jesus, even as family units. They sought the *touch* (verse 15) or blessing of Jesus upon even their infant children. This may have been due to a growing apprehension that Jesus might not be with them much longer. Since the common custom was for children to be seen and not heard, the attitude of the disciples is understandable. The prevalence of attention given by Jesus to children marked a higher value he afforded them by turning his back on custom. Also a new and wider dimension to the kingdom of God was unveiled as Jesus announced that the Kingdom belonged to them also (verse 16). It is the undiluted faith of a child which is essential for an adult also to *receive* and experience the fullness of the Kingdom (verse 17).

Self-denial Essential to Discipleship (18:18-30)

The first part of the verbal exchange between the ruler and Jesus revolves around the word *good* (verses 18-19). The ruler paid Jesus a high compliment by addressing him as *good teacher*, for he probably knew the customary outlook that only God had absolute goodness. All others were sinners. The ruler may have sensed divinity to be present in Jesus. Yet Jesus disclaimed the compliment; he saw it as belonging to God only.

The *eternal life* sought by the ruler was probably life with eternal or divine qualities permeating it. This was what he had seen in Jesus and he wanted it for himself. The traditional Jewish outlook was that the law, which was a revelation of God, gave life. Thus Jesus as a Jewish teacher referred his inquirer first to the Decalogue, or Ten Commandments, which were the heart of the law (verse 20). However, faithful obedience to the law had not brought life to this ruler.

Then Jesus pointed him to self-denial, a new dimension for discipleship. He was to sell and share earthly possessions (that is, to use what he had to meet the needs of others), and follow Jesus. He was to shut the door to what had been the center of his life and open the door to a new centerpiece. The result would be companionship with Christ here and eternal *treasure*, or life. However, he had become ensnared by his possessions and could not respond to Jesus' counsel (verse 23).

The humor of Jesus is evident in his word picture of a *camel* trying to *go through the eye of a needle* (verse 25). The absolute impossibility of it was a picture of how difficult it is for one whose life loyalties are wrapped around temporary riches rather than eternal purposes of God. Yet God can change, and save, even such a person (verse 27). Furthermore, as Jesus indicated to Peter, whatever is left behind for the sake of discipleship will be more than made up in what is to be received, when one looks at it from an eternal perspective (verses 29-30).

§ § § § § § §

The Message of Luke 17:1–18:30

In Luke 17:6 Jesus spoke of how faith even in small quantity could accomplish much. He used the figure of speech of uprooting a tree as an illustration of what might be accomplished. Faith was there identified as that which makes a difference in one's circumstances or surroundings. It is that which enables something to happen rather than something to be felt.

Although much of the various material in this section is not interrelated, we can find a common approach to these Scripture passages by discovering in them the traits for our life-style that the attitudes and life of faith should bring into existence. Looking panoramically at the passages we find a call for the following: forgiveness (17:3-4), gratitude (17:11-19), awareness of the Kingdom around us (17:20-21), watchfulness for the day of the Son of man yet to come (17:22-35), persistence in prayer (18:1-8), contrition (18:13-14), humility and receptivity (18:15-17), and sacrifice and commitment (18:18-30).

Each of us has tendencies within us to block the cultivation and possession of these virtues, such as spiritual stumbling blocks (17:1), hesitancy to forgive (17:3), ingratitude (17:16-18), spiritual indifference (17:27-28), momentary faith (18:8), spiritual pride (18:11-12), superiority (18:15), mixed loyalties (18:22), and possession-centeredness (18:23). Only through that form of faith that opens the door to God's operations and transformations within us, and the practice of faith that tackles the difficult and confronts that within us which is not in harmony with God's purposes for us, can this mountain be removed. Yet it can be, as Jesus affirmed, that *what is impossible with men is possible with God* (18:27).

§ § § § § § §

LUKE 18:31–19:44

Introduction to These Chapters

Both despair and hope are intermingled in this section
that records what happened as Jesus drew near to
Jerusalem, the object of his pilgrimage. The section
begins on a somber note as Jesus made clear his
impending rejection, torture, and death. Yet to a blind
man came sight and to a rich tax collector a new reason
for being and a new style of living—and teaching was
imparted on what should be done with what Jesus
brought. Then, coming full circle, the section ends on a
somber note with tears over Jerusalem's present and
future.

The section is divided into three parts.
  I. Warnings of What Lay Ahead (18:31-34)
 II. The Visit to Jericho (18:35-19:27)
III. The Ascent to Jerusalem (19:28-44)

Warnings of What Lay Ahead (18:31-34)

Since Jesus said, *We are going up to Jerusalem* (verse 31),
it can be presumed that he and the Twelve were in the
Jordan Valley, from which they would climb in altitude
to approach Jerusalem. Note that he said this to the
Twelve. It may have been his intention that they alone
accompany him on this last part of his journey.

Now Jesus clearly articulated what awaited him,
including a prediction of his death and resurrection

(verses 32-33). *Flogging* was done with an instrument consisting of three lashes made out of leather or small cords. On the end of these lashes sometimes sharp pieces of metal or bone were attached to increase the hurt they inflicted. In the light of the popularity of Jesus, the Twelve still could not believe that this would really happen and thus *they did not understand what was said* (verse 34).

The Visit in Jericho (18:35-19:27)

Jericho was a city seventeen miles east of Jerusalem near where the Jordan River enters the Dead Sea. It was located 820 feet below sea level. Jericho meant *place of fragrance*, perhaps because of the tropical growth there.

Son of David (verse 38) referred to Jesus being in the line of David (see 2:4), which was the line of messianic promise. The blind man calling Jesus by this title must have been Jewish, and familiar with the tradition of the messiah. The response of the people (verse 43) indicated that the popularity of Jesus had not waned. This is in contrast to the account in the Fourth Gospel where there is a growing disenchantment with Jesus.

Zacchaeus (19:2) is identified as a *chief tax collector.* This meant that he had administrative oversight over other tax collectors in the region. Because the collectors were known to retain part of the taxes they collected, Zacchaeus may well have accumulated for himself a portion of the collections of all the tax collectors under his jurisdiction. Thus he was rich. This was the second occasion when Jesus dined at the home of a tax collector, to the consternation of many onlookers (see 5:29-32).

Many tax collectors were drawn to Jesus for some unexplained reason. It may be that the word of his meal at Levi's house spread. Zacchaeus was obviously another one of them who was attracted by curiosity, and perhaps admiration, to hear Jesus. The strength of that interest is indicated by his climbing a tree to see Jesus (verse 4). The strong impression that Jesus made upon him is indicated by his profession of a changed lifestyle reflected in a generous sharing of possessions (verse 8).

Son of Abraham (verse 9) refers to his Jewish ancestry and his sharing that in common with Jesus. He had received the *salvation* promised to the Jews.

The supposition that the kingdom of God was to appear immediately may have been based upon the statements of Jesus recorded in 17:21 and 18:17. Another explanation would be that his audience presumed that Jesus would enter triumphantly into Jerusalem, demonstrate his messiahship, and claim the Kingdom for himself.

Some commentators maintain that the parable in verses 12-27 is based partly on an historical event. At the death of Herod the Great in 4 B.C., he left his kingdom divided between Herod Antipas, Herod Philip, and Archelaus, subject to Roman ratification. Archelaus, who inherited power over Judea, went to Rome to persuade Augustus to approve his rule over Judea. The Jews sent an embassy of fifty men to Rome to inform Augustus that they did not desire his kingship. However, Augustus did confirm him, but not with the title of king.

The coin referred to as a *pound* (verse 13, NRSV) was a Greek *mina* (NIV) worth about twenty dollars. In Matthew's account of this parable the amounts entrusted to the servants are much larger (Matthew 25:14-20).

The parable suggested to the disciples of Jesus their responsibility to make the most of what they have had the privilege to receive through Jesus. They had a stewardship and faithfulness to render. Jesus challenged them with this awareness as he moved toward the last week of his life.

The Ascent to Jerusalem (19:28-44)

Jesus now journeyed in reverse the road from Jerusalem to Jericho down which he had described the Good Samaritan traveling (10:30). Bethphage and Bethany were villages near Jerusalem and close to the Mount of Olives. *Bethphage* meant *house of figs* and *Bethany* meant *house of affliction.* In John's account (John 12:1) Bethany is identified as the home of Lazarus and his sisters.

Now the preparation for Jesus' entry into Jerusalem took place. First Jesus would ride upon an unbroken *colt* (verse 30) in the spirit of Zechariah 9:9. Being the first to ride upon it would be a symbol of his uniqueness as Messiah. With their garments they made a royal covering over the colt as a seat for Jesus. Then they spread their garments on the road as a carpet for royalty (verse 36). This was a custom when a king was anointed, such as Jehu (2 Kings 9:13). In Luke's account this series of events took place as Jesus approached the city rather than as he entered the city.

The words of praise and identification in verse 38 are echoes of Psalm 118:26. In his earlier lament over Jerusalem (13:34-35), Jesus had ended by announcing that those in Jerusalem would not see him until they said *Blessed be he who comes in the name of the Lord! Peace in heaven and glory in the highest* (verse 38) is reminiscent of the anthem of the heavenly host at Jesus' birth (2:14).

The call of the Pharisees to Jesus to rebuke your disciples was because they felt it was inappropriate, even blasphemous, for them to be conducting a public demonstration with shouted designations of Jesus as Messiah (verse 39). In response, Jesus used a figure of speech from the prophet Habakkuk (Habakkuk 2:11*a*).

A second time Jesus lamented over the city of Jerusalem (verse 41). Jesus employed a play on words as he expressed a wish that those in Jerusalem knew the things that make for peace (verse 42). The word *Jerusalem* meant *house of peace* or *abode of peace.* The place of peace would miss its true peace. Jesus' despair was deepened by an awareness that Jerusalem itself would be destroyed (verses 33-34). In A.D. 70 the city was laid waste by the Romans under Titus at the height of enmity between Jews and Romans. The irony was that the city in which efforts would be undertaken to destroy Jesus would itself be destroyed.

§ § § § § § §

The Message of Luke 18:31–19:44

Jesus went to Jerusalem out of commitment to God and to people. As this section reveals, Jesus continued to make his witness and carry out his ministry on the way and after he arrived.

Why did he go to Jerusalem? Obviously he knew, in large measure, what awaited him. The largest portion of Luke's narrative relates in some manner to Jerusalem. As early as 9:51 Luke states of Jesus that *he set his face to go to Jerusalem*. The remainder of the narrative describes events and sayings that took place on the journey there or while there.

This focus on Jerusalem seems important to Luke because the messiah was to appear there, according to the prophetic tradition. Keeping the Jerusalem destination in the foreground reinforced the image of Jesus as Messiah.

Toward this city representing the might of God and humanity, Jesus set his face. Practically, Jesus would have known that for his truth to make a big difference in society, it would have to make an impact upon the powers that determined the fate of God's children (such as Zacchaeus). As Messiah he would have to witness to that fact by his very presence in Jerusalem.

As a Jew who sought to enliven his religious tradition while living out that tradition, making change from within rather than from without, Jesus would make a pilgrimage to Jerusalem, especially to be there for the Passover. And if he had new truth to share about God, he would have to share it where God was even seen to dwell. As Paul after him felt about Rome, Jesus could not be content until he had witnessed at Jerusalem.

§ § § § § § §

LUKE 19:45–21:38

Introduction to These Chapters

Jesus has arrived at Jerusalem and entered the city. We
now enter with Jesus into the last week in his life. This
section includes those passages which report teachings
and events that took place during the first half of that
week. As to location, the primary focus is the Temple. As
for the teachings, they primarily deal with basics, such as
the purpose and future of the Temple, the nature of
Jesus' authority and role, the nature of life beyond life,
and the last days. The section includes the following
components:

I. Confrontations in the Temple (19:45–20:8)
II. Parable on Spiritual Irresponsibility (20:9-18)
III. Plotting by Questioning (20:19-26)
IV. Dialogue on Life After Death (20:27-40)
V. Commentary on Messiahship (20:41-44)
VI. Genuineness Contrasted with Pretense (20:45–21:4)
VII. Impermanence of All Except Faith (21:5-36)
VIII. Jesus' Daily Patterns (21:37-38)

Confrontations in the Temple (19:45–20:8)

For the Jew there was no place more sacred for
worship or more significant in history than the Temple in
Jerusalem. Its creation had been the fulfillment of
generations of hopes and its preservation and restoration
had repeatedly been a matter of concern and effort. Each
Jew sought to worship and offer sacrifices in the Temple
as often as possible, and at least once a year. Those who

lived in distant places would try to make a pilgrimage to the Temple at least once in their lifetime. Although such pilgrimages and worship could take place at any time, the preferred time was during the feast of the Passover, the most important of all Jewish festival or ritual occasions. Josephus, the Jewish historian, supports an estimate that more than 100,000 pilgrims might well have been in the city at that time. Thus it was in keeping with this perspective that Jesus now made his way to Jerusalem and the Temple.

Since sacrifices were to be offered as a part of the worship ritual, birds and animals were sold at the Temple for this purpose to avoid the necessity of bringing them long distances. Also, such sacrificial animals required inspection by the priests to certify that they were without blemish. However, the cost of these items was inflated in order to provide income for the seller and the Temple hierarchy. Often there was loud haggling over the prices between worshipers and sellers. It had become a commercial enterprise, exploiting the poor to the advantage of the Temple superiors. Thus Jesus *began to drive out those who were selling* (verse 45).

The statement by Jesus in verse 46 is a combination of quotations from Isaiah 56:7 and Jeremiah 7:11.

For Jesus to teach daily *in the temple* (verse 47) was an act of bravado and faithful witness in the light of the currents of objection by religious leaders and warnings of death previously received. Yet he was fulfilling the role of being God's spokesperson. Interestingly, early in his life story, as a child, he had been *in the temple, sitting among the teachers, listening to them and asking them questions* (2:46). Now, in the last phase of his life, he was back in the Temple as a teacher himself. Just as he had been an intense listener then as a lad, now *the people hung upon his words* (verse 48, NIV; NRSV = *were spellbound*).

His challenge of the Temple's economic practices and his teaching as a rabbi or prophet in the Temple were more than could be accepted by the *chief priest, scribes,* and *leaders* (verse 47), and his destruction was, to them, a necessity. This resulted in the confrontation described in verses 20:1-8. Viewing Jesus as presumptuous, they asked for his *authority* or credentials for what he did and proclaimed. He answered with the question about John the Baptist (verse 4) and John's authority in baptizing. If they said that John had divine authority (*from heaven*), then they would be subject to criticism for failing to believe John. If they said it was only a human initiative, then they would be subject to violent reactions. For John was now regarded even more highly because of his martyrdom in response to his statements of conviction against the Roman rulers with which the Jewish populace agreed. Since they said they did not know, Jesus refused to state his authority.

Parable on Spiritual Irresponsibility (20:9-18)

Once again Jesus taught through a parable, with its setting being a vineyard and its characters being an owner and tenants or servants (see 12:36-40; 16:1-9; 19:11-26). In the parable there is a presumption by the tenants that because they had continually been successful in rejecting the emissaries of the owner, they would always be successful. This became evident in their attitude that they could obtain the land for themselves by killing the son and heir (verse 14). This would lead the owner to give up and accede to their occupation. However, they did not count on the owner being persistent in his intentions, to which he gave expression by destroying *those tenants* and giving the vineyard to others.

This parable needs to be seen in the light of its having been spoken during the last week in Jesus' life and as a supplement to the parable about the pounds offered by Jesus as he approached Jerusalem (19:11-26).

He called for the people to recall the words in Psalm 118:22 (which Luke also uses in his account about Jesus in Acts 4:11). The *stone,* which undoubtedly is Christ, the Messiah, can be constructive (verse 17), like a cornerstone for a building. Or it can be destructive (verse

18) when evil ones stumble in confrontation with him or are *crushed* when Christ shares in the ultimate judgment.

Plotting by Questioning (20:19-26)

The scribes (NRSV; NIV = *teachers of the law*) *and the chief priests* (verse 19) sensed that they were being identified as the *tenants* in the preceding parable. They had rejected God's son and would be *destroyed.* Incensed, they *tried to lay hands on him* (NRSV; NIV = *to arrest him*) but held off because of the admiration of *the people* for Jesus. The *spies* (verse 20) were sent to listen to him and catch him in some statement of rebellion or challenge to Roman authority. Then Jesus could have been reported to the Roman governor, Pontius Pilate, who would have had him seized. This would have accomplished their purpose without a direct confrontation between these Jewish leaders and the people.

Taxes (verse 22) refers to an annual poll tax collected from every adult male for the Roman government. *Caesar* was the title of the emperor of the Roman Empire. Archelaus had established this requirement in Judea in A.D. 6. It was a very unpopular tax and an additional tax burden. By asking Jesus whether he felt it was *lawful* (NRSV; NIV = *right*) to pay this tax, the spies were hoping to trick him into saying what the people felt and would like to hear, that this tax was unjust and should not be paid. Then they could report him to the Roman authorities as disloyal and urging disloyalty. But Jesus perceived their intent (verse 23). Mark used the word translated *hypocrisy* (Mark 12:15) to describe their nature.

The inscription of the Caesar was customarily placed upon a Roman coin in the same way it would be done with a present-day president, king, or queen. In this statement, *Give to Caesar the things that are Caesar's, and to God the things that are God's* (verse 25, NIV), Jesus pointed out a dual obligation of his hearers to the government and the religious tradition. Each must decide what was due and owed to each. Even his enemies were amazed at the shrewdness of his answer.

Dialogue on Life After Death (20:27-40)

The Sadducees were another group within the Jewish religious tradition. The name was derived from Zadok, the priest during David's reign (2 Samuel 8:17). The Sadducees saw authority in the Scripture only and not in the teachings of the elders, and held to the right of private interpretation of Scripture. They differed from the Pharisees also in that they believed that the soul died with the body and there was no resurrection. Also they did not believe in angels or spirits. They tended to be more adaptable to life and customs around them. They shared with the Pharisees in membership in the Sanhedrin, the ruling body of Judaism.

The Mosaic law summarized in verse 28 appears in Deuteronomy 25:5-6 and is known as the levirate marriage law. It called on a brother to take responsibility for the widow of his brother and enable her to have children if she was childless.

In answering the question regarding an extreme case of multiple mates, Jesus alluded to an entirely different form of life in the resurrected state (verse 35), where ordinary human forms and marital customs do not apply. Their status is like that of *angels* and ageless children of God. Since there is no death, there is no need for the creation of children to preserve one's family lineage.

The reference to Moses in verse 37 alludes to the experience of his calling in the wilderness (see Exodus 3). There God used the identification of *God of Abraham, the God of Isaac, and the God of Jacob* (Exodus 3:6). Jesus used this reference to indicate that God could be the God of all three at the same time only if two of them were continuing to live by having been raised from the dead.

Commentary on Messiahship (20:41-44)

This strange commentary of Jesus is an analysis of Psalm 110:1. At first reading, it appears that Jesus was denying his ancestral descent from David. However, notice that Jesus here used the title *Christ* (verse 41, NIV; NRSV-*Messiah*) in the discussion. It was about the messiah that he was speaking. Psalm 110 was probably not originally written to speak of the messiah but of an earthly king. However, time, together with the desire for the messiah, had led many to see this psalm as having a double reference: to a king and the messiah (who would be like a king). Thus as Jesus quoted the psalm, the second use of the word *Lord* was seen by many as a reference to the messiah. In this light the quotation suggested that the messiah was *Lord,* or more than merely a descendant of David.

Genuineness Compared to Pretense (20:45-21:4)

Jesus was probably still at the Temple when he commented on the *scribes* (NRSV; NIV = *teachers of the law*). (For an explanation of the scribes see the commentary on 5:30.) It was a daring statement to be made in *the hearing of all the people* (verse 45). The *long robes* were the robes of a teacher or rabbi. Rabbis were held in great respect in the Jewish tradition—given deference in public, called "master" in conversation, and seated up front in the special seats facing the congregation in the synagogue. They were supposed to support themselves financially by a trade and take nothing for teaching. Yet among their ranks were those who took as much as they could from any source, including the very limited resources of *widows* (verse 47). Because a widow had a special place of respect and protection under the Jewish law (see Exodus 22:22), this practice was especially offensive.

The episode of the giving of the *poor widow* is a sequel to the preceding observation and a contrast to his appraisal of the scribes. The widow, who received the teaching of the scribes and was victimized by some of them, was rated higher in the eyes of Jesus than the scribes themselves. While they selfishly took for themselves, the widow gave sacrificially.

There were thirteen trumpet-shaped receptacles, each for a different purpose, in an area of the Temple called the *treasury* (verse 1). This would have been at or near the Court of Women, for women did not have access to all areas of the Temple. The *two copper coins* (verse 2) would have been leptons, the smallest in value of Jewish coins. The name meant *the thin one.* To have contributed *all the living that she had* would mean all she had to live on for that day.

Impermanence of All Except Faith (21:5-36)

This conversation, which begins with a comment on the bejeweled splendor of the Temple, may appear here as a reaction of contrast to the *poor widow's* circumstances.

The Temple is described as *adorned with beautiful stones and gifts* (verse 5). The ornateness of the Temple was well known, and was a sight that many traveled to see. For detailed descriptions of all the wood carvings, precious metals and metalwork, and gems included in the design and construction, which extended eleven years under Solomon, see 1 Kings 6–7. The front wall of the Temple was covered with gold plates that reflected the brilliance of the sun at sunrise.

The destruction of this spiritual center and architectural showplace was predicted by Jesus, to the certain shock and dismay of his hearers. The Temple, having been destroyed once before, was seen as even more permanent now. The thought of a second destruction would be horrendous, and almost considered blasphemous. Yet the Temple was burned in A.D. 70 and its walls knocked down as a part of the destruction of the city by the Romans in reaction to Jewish revolt and attitudes toward Rome.

The warning in verse 8 is against false messiahs. *Wars and revolutions* (NIV; NRSV = *insurrections*) mentioned in verse 9 were among the traditional *signs* of the coming of the Day of the Lord. This is also true of the events listed in verses 10-11. *Pestilences* (NIV; NRSV = *plagues*) were epidemic diseases, often with widespread fatalities. *Fearful events* (NIV; NRSV = *dreadful portents*) *and great signs from heaven* could be meteorites, lightning displays, or such events in the sky.

The persecution, imprisonment, and suffering that Jesus had predicted for himself (18:31-34) was now presented as the fate for his disciples (verses 12-13). Yet with the dire predictions were always given encouraging promises (*I will give you words and wisdom*, verse 15; *not a hair of your head will perish*, verse 18). Jesus warns that discipleship does not exempt one from threat or even harm, but still God never forsakes the people.

As previously stated in the commentary on verse 6, the *armies* (verse 20) of Rome would bring about the *desolation* of Jerusalem, which results in the warnings in verse 21. Those who are pregnant and those with newborns (*nursing*) will be especially vulnerable. They will have feelings of hopelessness for their children, because the destruction will spare no one and the captivity or enslavement might come to anyone then. *Until the times of the Gentiles are fulfilled* means until the time of vengeance or judgment upon the Jews through non-Jews (the Romans) has ended.

The coming of the Day of the Lord was to be preceded by cosmic and natural events, as previously stated (see verses 10-11). Jesus now adopted those signs as potential signs for the coming of the *Son of man* with the implication that he was the fulfillment of that title. Again, in the midst of calamity, Jesus called them to *look up* (verse 28) beyond those calamities with the awareness that *your redemption is drawing near.* The Greek word translated *redemption* comes from a verb meaning *to release on payment of ransom.* It can be translated also as *deliverance* or *liberation.*

This parable of the fig tree (verses 29-31) may not be located in its proper place in the narrative. Its theme is the *kingdom of God* drawing hear, while the teachings preceding and following it focus on the coming of the Son of man. It would fit in better as a companion piece to earlier teachings on the Kingdom (such as following 17:21). This parable tends to reinforce the sense of the nearness and immediacy of the Kingdom in the same way Jesus had earlier suggested that in his present coming the Kingdom had drawn near.

However, some had seen the coming of the Kingdom and the coming of the Son of man as simultaneous or identical. This may explain the parable being located here. There was a growing sense that, if Jesus was put to death, he would return in some form and this would happen soon (verse 32), and that this would be another manifestation of the kingdom of God.

In verses 34-36 Jesus returned to the theme of watchfulness that he earlier urged (12:45-47) in the light of God's interventions at any time.

The *fig tree* (verse 29) was very common in Palestine. (See also 13:6-9.) The budding (*leaf*) of the tree occurred in the spring in advance of the fruit that appeared in the summer.

Jesus' Daily Patterns (21:37-38)

During this week in Jerusalem, Jesus spent the larger portion of his time teaching in the Temple, from early morning until evening. There seemed a sense of urgency on his part to teach as much as he could to as many as he could while he could. There also appeared to be an equal eagerness and urgency on the part of many people to hear him. These prolonged periods of teaching within the Temple also reinforced his status as a rabbi, if not as a prophet also.

At the same time, retreat to privacy for prayer, recollection, and rest continued as a part of his daily pattern (verse 37), as it had been periodically all along, from the beginning of his ministry (4:42).

§ § § § § § §

The Message of Luke 19:45–21:38

The materials that are recorded in this section of Luke's account have a common locale, the Temple; but they touch on many different subjects. Yet interwoven beneath them all is a consistent attempt on the part of Jesus to encourage his hearers to distinguish the eternal in the midst of the temporal, that which is of true value amidst momentary impressiveness.

For instance, Jesus came to the centerpiece of the Jewish spiritual tradition, the Temple, along with multitudes of other faithful pilgrims. Yet he announced the impermanence and even the destruction of the Temple. Thus he proclaimed that one's faith must be centered not in impermanent buildings to house God, but in the eternal personhood of God (21:6). While acknowledging an obligation to the governing power, Jesus affirmed an equal obligation to God (20:25). He pointed out that life in God is longer and transcends human relationships (20:38). A widow's sacrificial giving far exceeds in authentic spiritual value the pious customs of the formally religious. Hardship and persecution and participation in calamities await the Christian disciple, but God's providential protection and deliverance will be equally present.

The net result is a renewed call for watchfulness. This call is not just to be watchful and spiritually prepared for the coming of the Son of man, but also to be watchful for the eternal in the midst of the temporal, and the spiritually genuine in the midst of the synthetic.

§ § § § § § §

Introduction to These Verses

In this section of Luke's narrative, Jesus moves toward the last mile of the way, and in preparation comes face to face with the realities of his own somber predictions. It is Jesus' last time with his disciples before his arrest and death. It begins with preparations for the last supper, ends at the high priest's house, and includes the following:

   I. Covenant of Betrayal (22:1-6)
   II. The Last Supper (22:7-38)
   III. Prayer at Olivet (22:39-46)
   IV. Betrayal and Arrest (22:47-54)

Covenant of Betrayal (22:1-6)

The *feast of Unleavened Bread* (verse 1) and the Passover were two different commemorative events prescribed by the Mosaic law (see Leviticus 23:4-7) that were interrelated. Both were intended to recall aspects of God's deliverance of the Jews from Egypt.

The Passover recalled the "passing over" of the Jewish families by the angel of death, who came as the last of the plagues against Pharaoh and Egypt, and the special meal eaten on that occasion (see Exodus 12:1-32). These families were to place some blood from a sacrificed lamb on the doorposts of their houses. The angel passed over such houses and their firstborn children were spared. In commemoration and gratitude an evening Passover meal was to be observed on the fourteenth day of the first month of the Jewish year, called Nisan (see Exodus 13:3-10). In remembrance of the sacrifice of lambs at the time of the angel's visitation in Egypt, the sacrifice of a lamb was called for in preparation for the Passover meal. It was called the paschal lamb.

The Jews were instructed to eat the sacrificed animal with unleavened cakes, since they did not have time to leaven the bread in that original meal because it had to be eaten *in haste* (Exodus 12:11, 39). This unleavened bread was to be eaten for seven days, thus creating the feast of Unleavened Bread. This feast began on the fifteenth day of Nisan and lasted seven days; on the seventh day a holy convocation was to be held (Leviticus 13:5-7).

Apparently from Luke's perspective the religious authorities felt that they had sufficient evidence in hand of blasphemy by Jesus to bring formal charges against him which could result in a death sentence, if the Roman authority consented. This would also get rid of Jesus as a threat. So now the dilemma was not whether to charge him but where and how to seize him. Jesus obviously still stood high in public favor, and this had been a continuing threat and frustration to their intents and plans this week (19:47-48; 20:26).

Evil intent was seen as produced by evil spirits. Thus *Satan* (meaning *adversary* or, in the Hebrew, *obstruct*), the chief of devils and evil itself, was seen as entering *into Judas* to make him susceptible to being used for betrayal. The *officers* (verse 4) would have been officers of the Jewish guard, for the Romans had not yet become involved. To be able to seize Jesus *when no crowd was present* (verse 6) was what was sought by the Jewish authorities and what would be provided by Judas. Judas would notify them where and when he would be in a secluded setting with few persons around him.

Beyond the explanation of evil influence and the possible implication of monetary gain, Luke gives no

reason for the willingness of Judas to betray Jesus. Some
surmise that Judas wanted to force the hand of Jesus—to
make him assume authority as Messiah, which direct
confrontation with the Jewish authorities might
stimulate. Others sense that Judas might have become
disillusioned with Jesus' idealism in contrast with his
own practical (and perhaps material) priorities.

The Last Supper (22:7-38)

Jesus told Peter and John to *enter the city* (verse 10),
thus implying that these instructions were given while
they were at the Mount of Olives, where they were
spending the nights during their stay in Jerusalem (21:37).

The *Passover lamb* (verse 7) was sacrificed on the
afternoon prior to the evening Passover meal.

One highly speculative tradition suggests that the *large
upper room furnished* (verse 12) may have been in the
house of John Mark's mother, where the disciples would
later gather after the Resurrection (Acts 1:13). This would
mean that the *man carrying a jar of water* could have been
Mark, and *the owner of the house* Mark's father. Rooms for
meals would have been especially scarce during the
Passover observance, so Jesus and his group would have
needed to make advance arrangements (verse 12).

There is substantial uncertainty as to whether this
supper described by Luke was really the Passover meal
or the Passover eve meal. In the Fourth Gospel, John
speaks of it as taking place the day before the Passover
(John 18:28; 19:14, 31, 42). This fits more logically into the
schedule of events that took place after the meal. If this
actually was the Passover meal, it would mean that Jesus
was betrayed, arrested, tried, sentenced, and crucified on
Passover, which extended from sunset to sunset. Because
Passover was such a sacred observance, the Sabbath
restrictions would ordinarily pertain to it also, which
would preclude such as that which happened to Jesus.

The selected group of *apostles* (verse 14; 6:13-16) were

the guests at the dinner. Jesus began by stressing his desire to eat this meal with them. His focus was upon the group itself and his yearning for this experience of fellowship. The use of *eagerly* represents the intensity of the desire, as is explicit in the Greek wording. The first aspect of this meal was a communion with each other.

To eat the meal when it is fulfilled *in the kingdom of God* (verse 16) means to dine at the promised banquet in the kingdom of God or messianic celebration (see Luke 14:15-24). In Luke's account the *cup* is offered first, probably because at the Passover meal the custom was to have on the table a cup of the fruit of the vine and a loaf of bread. The host would take a cup or goblet of the *fruit of the vine* (verse 18) and offer a blessing over it. This would be a prayer of gratitude to God for life and sustenance which had permitted celebration of this festival. There was also an affirmation of praise to God for the wine. He would then pass it to others present to drink, or pour into their own individual receptacles. The allusion here to the coming of the *kingdom of God* as the setting for his future partaking may refer to the Resurrection.

In the biblical tradition, breaking bread had spiritual symbolism. Bread represented the providence of God. The elements in bread provided vital substances the human body needed. When bread was broken and shared with others it was a sharing of essentials, what was necessary for life to continue. Jesus chose bread to represent himself, his body, as a similar value and essential for the spiritual nourishment of his followers.

The presence of a betrayer, although not named (verses 21-22), is acknowledged. This must have caused shock and dismay to these apostles—both the announcement of betrayal and that it would come from their midst. They searched among themselves for the culprit.

What a startling contrast then took place! They moved from a search among themselves for the betrayer to a search for *the greatest* (verse 24). The former search was distasteful; the latter search was disappointing. Again Jesus must redefine *greatness* to his apostles, as he had done much earlier for his disciples (9:46-48) when they had had a similar dispute. How disappointing it must have been in these last moments of Jesus' life for him to have to still be teaching basics to his chosen intimates—that spiritual greatness is not defined in terms of prestige and authority but in the attitude and offering of humble service (verses 25-27).

In the midst of the meal Jesus spoke of those about the table as *those who have stood by me in my trials* (verse 28) and will *eat and drink at my table in my kingdom* (verse 30) with strategic tasks of spiritual responsibility. This last supper bound together those around the table in a new recognition of God's presence in their midst, God's providence in their lives, and their own spiritual bonds with one another. Jesus wanted his disciples to recognize those bonds and to find a new commitment to reach out to one another. He needed them and they needed him. This communion would sustain them in the hours ahead.

This became even more evident in the dialogue with Simon Peter (verses 31-34). Then Jesus identified the struggle awaiting him, but affirmed his support and confidence in him and urged him to use the struggle as stimulus to help others caught up in such *sifting.* In sifting wheat through a sieve, one removed the waste from the genuine grains. So Simon was to be tried, which would determine what was only pretense or what was genuine about his commitment. Interestingly, the pronoun *you* when first used in verse 31 is plural in the Greek text, but becomes singular in verse 32. Perhaps Jesus was talking to Simon but saying that all around the table were sought by Satan. Each would be put through a sifting process in the days ahead, through which they and those around them would discover who they were and what was the nature of their faith commitment.

Peter's affirmation of his allegiance (verse 33) would come back to haunt him. The sifting process was about to begin, and he would fail Jesus three times before the next sunrise, or when the cock crows (verse 34).

The sending out (verse 35) had first taken place (10:1-16) immediately after *he set his face to go to Jerusalem* (9:51). After his arrest and sentence to death as a *transgressor* (verse 37, [NIV; NRSV = *lawless*]—a quotation from Isaiah 53:12), his followers would be at greater risk and amidst less popularity and support. No longer would they be able to count on others to provide them support or protection.

Prayer at Olivet (22:39-46)

The daily retreat to the Mount of Olives (verse 39) was now an accustomed pattern (19:37; 21:37). The Mount, which was a chain of hills, was opposite the eastern walls of Jerusalem.

The *temptation* (verse 40, NIV; NRSV = *the time of trial*) which was to be an object of prayer may well have been the temptation to forsake their commitment to Jesus when the impending arrest and trial took place. This would be part of the sifting process. Jesus could be empathetic with his disciples at this point because he himself was struggling with his own commitment to God's purpose and plan for himself (verses 42-44).

The *cup* was the cup of suffering. Earlier in the evening he had shared his cup with others (verse 17). That image was fresh in his mind and now he used it in prayer as he envisioned the cup God wanted him to share. While God called for him to drink that cup, God reached out to strengthen him through *an angel* (verse 43).

Other gospel accounts describe Jesus praying three times. Luke simply says, *He prayed more earnestly.* The intensity of the struggle of the hour is evident not only by his perspiring, but also that sweat becoming as blood (verse 44).

In contrast the disciples were *sleeping* (verse 45). However, lest they be condemned too quickly, the Greek word translated *sorrow* refers to pain of body or mind that results in grief or sorrow. They may have been emotionally exhausted by the sinister turn of events and the sense of an impending loss. The disciples needed to pray, however, for the shadows of *temptation* (verse 46, NIV; NRSV = *the time of trial*) were already falling upon the Mount.

Betrayal and Arrest (22:47-54)

The *crowd* may have been a large group of Jewish soldiers and servants recruited by the authorities for fear that they might encounter violent resistance to Jesus' arrest. What Judas had promised as a form of betrayal was the location and time where Jesus could be taken with minimum public note, and also to identify in the dark of the night for the soldiers which person was Jesus. This he would do with a kiss (verse 48). That act would not be unusual, since in the East disciples would kiss their teacher or rabbi, thus showing tribute and affection. Jesus' use of the title *Son of man* as he responded to Judas reminded him that the betrayal was not just that of a human hero but God's promised and anointed servant.

Since Jesus had earlier in the evening indicated that they might have a future need for a sword (verses 36-38), one disciple (named as Peter in John 18:10-11) sensed that this was the time and took a sword to injure one of the high priest's slaves. But Jesus rebuked this hurt and violence, even though the crowd was apparently well armed *with swords and clubs* (verse 52). Jesus was aware of the reason they had chosen the night to seize him, but he taunted them with the rhetorical question in verse 52. This was the *power of darkness* (NRSV; NIV = *when darkness reigns*) at work and best done in a dark hour.

For a midnight hearing they took Jesus to the house of the high priest rather than to the usual hearing chambers at the Temple complex.

§ § § § § § §

The Message of Luke 22:1-54

Jesus had the ability to use simple images to reveal deep and important truths. He did this often in his teaching, using as object lessons a lamp, a coin, birds, seeds, and even a colt. At this last supper he taught in a memorable way with cup and bread. These simple, everyday items Jesus forever filled with special meaning by injecting himself into them. In this ceremony the material and spiritual came together as tradition and immediacy also merged. These physical items became a part of the bloodstream and cells of those partaking; they became part of those persons.

Just as these items enter into our bodies and become part of us, so Christ enters into us by his spirit and becomes part of us. The Lord's Supper becomes not just communion with a memory but an avenue for a new entrance of Christ into us.

Then through our life Christ moves out into the life of the world. It may be into a night of darkness and struggle as on the Mount of Olives. It may be into a confrontation with *principalities and powers and spiritual wickedness,* such as awaited the disciples. If we can be watchful, God will send us the resources to strengthen us as we struggle to align our wills with God's purposes for us, and allow Christ to live through us.

We are overwhelmed by his gracious acceptance, forgiveness, and promise. They turn us around. Then we move into our world of sinister shadows, frustrated hopes, and sweaty prayers, aware of his presence within us, and of his life to be lived through us, and of his love for others to be shared by us, even as we have received it. And we realize we have been converted.

§ § § § § § §

Introduction to These Chapters

The day of infamy was at hand. Jesus had entered into the "lonesome valley." He had to walk it all by himself. Separated from the support, which was weak in part, of the disciples, and away from the supportive crowds, Jesus was alone with accusers and opponents in a legal process with a fixed aim: his death. Then the death march was undertaken and the throes of a criminal execution experienced. It was the last mile of the way, with these markers en route.

I. Peter's Denials (22:55-62)
II. The Preliminary Hearing (22:63-71)
III. Hearing Before Pilate (23:1-25)
IV. Procession to Calvary (23:26-32)
V. Crucifixion (23:33-49)

Peter's Denials (22:55-62)

Nights in the Middle East can be cool, particularly at the altitude at which Jerusalem is located. Thus it would be natural for there to have been a fire in the courtyard (verse 55) for the soldiers or servants to warm themselves in the middle of this night. Peter, who had come behind those who arrested Jesus, having been on the Mount of Olives all evening, also sought the warmth of the fire. The firelight illumined Peter's face in the darkness and made him recognizable. This led to three accusations by onlookers that he was among the disciples of Jesus present with him at his arrest (verses 56-60). To all, Peter denied the relationship. He began his denials as he sought physical comfort and continued with them until they became an accustomed response.

The third accuser suspected Peter because he appeared or talked as a resident of Galilee (*Galilean,* verse 59). Jesus was known to have been from Galilee. The *rooster crowed* (verse 60), and at that point Jesus was visible as he was being moved from one place to another. His eyes caught Peter's eyes. Together they brought to Peter the startling reawareness of Jesus' disturbing prediction of these denials even when Peter was affirming his willingness to go *to prison and to death* (22:33). Stricken and guilty in spirit, *he went out and wept bitterly* (verse 62).

The Preliminary Hearing (22:63-71)

The abuse given to Jesus was both physical (*beat him*) and mental (*mocked him*) (verse 63). The mockery was an attempt to ridicule him. One form it took was to make fun of his reputed role as a prophet and seer. This was why they *blindfolded him* (verse 64) and then asked him to identify the one who beat him.

Luke does not provide the name of the person holding this first hearing. His account suggests that Jesus was taken to a high priest's house in the middle of the night. Then in the morning Jesus was taken before the chief priests and Sanhedrin. The account in John's Gospel reports that Jesus was first taken to Annas, who was the predecessor of Caiaphas, then high priest, and also his father-in-law (John 18:13). Thus it may be that in Luke's account it was to the residence of Annas that Jesus was first taken for an inquiry and holding until the morning, giving time for the Sanhedrin to be gathered. Then Caiaphas, the high priest, would have presided over the hearing by the *council* (NIV; NRSV = *assembly*) or Sanhedrin (verse 66). A nighttime trial was not legal. But if the hearing could be held early, then they could get

Jesus into the hands of the Romans before the general public would be aware and initiate any protest. (For a more extensive account of the hearing before Caiaphas, see Mark 4:53-65.)

The council was the Jewish governing body that carried jurisdiction over Jewish affairs, as authorized by the Romans. It was called the Sanhedrin, which was a transliteration of the Greek word meaning *council*. The Sanhedrin in Jerusalem carried authority for all Judea and the surrounding area, as determined by Caesar in 47 B.C. It consisted of seventy members, corresponding to the seventy elders appointed by Moses to assist him as judges, plus the high priest. It had a police force of servants under its jurisdiction. Later other disciples and early church leaders would be summoned before the council (see Acts 4:5-6; 5:21-41; 6:12; 22:30, for example). Its members had the authority to determine most civil and religious issues and punishments. But they could not order the death sentence. They could recommend such, but the Roman authority had to confirm a sentence of death.

The plan was to prove and accuse Jesus as guilty of blasphemy. This intention underlay the content of the questioning. They first wanted to know if Jesus claimed to be the Christ, or Messiah. He did not answer their question directly, but in his response used the title *Son of man*, with an inference that he was that person of divine promise, yet to be demonstrated in fact. They then asked the most sensitive question of all: *Are you the Son of God?* (verse 70). Jesus' answer is subject to varying translations of the Greek text. It could be *You are right. I am.* In any event, his hearers interpreted his response as affirmative. *What further testimony do we need?* (verse 71, NRSV).

To the Roman authority, Pontius Pilate, Jesus would now be taken with an accusation and a recommendation that he deserved a sentence of death.

Hearing Before Pilate (23:1-25)

Pontius Pilate was the Roman procurator or governor of Judea from A.D. 26 to 36. He was immensely unpopular with the Jews because he had permitted his troops to carry ensigns with images of the emperor on them into Jerusalem and had taken sacred Temple money to build a water conduit. However, the Jews had no choice but to go through him to obtain a death sentence. Ordinarily, the procurator would be at his official residence on the coast at Caesarea, but he would be in Jerusalem when the great Jewish festivals were observed to be certain that law and order were maintained.

The whole assembly went to Pilate, meaning that most of the Sanhedrin went to strengthen their appeal. The setting would probably have been the royal palace built by Herod the Great, located on a hill southwest of the Temple mount, when he was king of Judea. There was no king now, and Pilate ruled as such, using this palace when in Jerusalem. The charges presented were cast in such a form as to prejudice Pilate against Jesus from the beginning: subversion, disloyalty, and proclaiming himself a king (verse 2).

Although the Mosaic law called for the death of a blasphemer, a Roman ruler would not take very seriously a controversy over religious ideas, and would not approve such a sentence. Thus the charges had to be recast into a form that would get his very serious attention—namely, a threat to Rome. Of course, the second charge, *forbidding us to pay taxes to Caesar,* would have been obviously false in the light of Luke's account of Jesus saying the opposite in 20:25. *Tribute* meant taxes.

Pilate zeroed in immediately on what was the most threatening of the charges to Rome: Jesus identifying himself as a king. To Pilate's question, Jesus gave a strangely worded response: *You say so* (verse 3, NRSV; NIV—*it is as you say*). What Jesus was probably saying was that the words proclaiming him as a king came from others and were repeated in Pilate's question. He had made no such proclamation about himself.

Perhaps sensing this matter to be one of trivial religious jealousy or not wishing to spend time with the matter, Pilate responded, *I find no basis to charge this man* (verse 4). In the intense discontent with his appraisal expressed by the council, they declared his influence to be troublesome in all the area as far away as Galilee (verse 5). Pilate picked up on this and learned that Jesus was from Galilee. Pilate's jurisdiction extended only throughout Judea. The ruler of Galilee also happened to be in Jerusalem for the celebrations. This gave Pilate a way out of a delicate and tense situation.

So he referred the case to Herod Antipas, then ruler of Galilee. The Herods were a dynasty that ruled Galilee for several generations. Already Luke has reported the curiosity of Herod Antipas about Jesus (see the commentary on 9:7-9) and the warning of some Pharisees to Jesus that Herod wanted to kill him (13:31). Jesus had even sent a message to Herod in response (13:32-33). This is the background for Luke's observation that Herod was very glad to question Jesus because *for a long time he had been wanting to see him* (verse 8). Apparently Herod's dominant impression of Jesus from rumors he had received was that of a miracle worker or a doer of unusual deeds. He wanted to see Jesus "perform" firsthand.

To Herod's questioning Jesus *gave no answer* (verse 9). This could have been a witness of contempt by Jesus toward Herod, who had put John the Baptist to death, or a refusal on the part of Jesus to cooperate with Herod's intentions to see Jesus in action. Only the Jewish leaders came to this hearing, but they presented the charges *vehemently*. Since Jesus showed contempt for Herod, Herod showed contempt and frustration toward Jesus by making fun of his so-called kingly status with rude and scornful acts and adorning him with a mock-royal robe.

The nature and cause of the enmity between Herod and Pilate (verse 12) is not known.

For the second time Pilate had Jesus on his hands. This time he called for *the people* (verse 13) to attend the hearing also. This may simply refer to the Sanhedrin, who had been present at his earlier hearing. If it was an invitation to the general public, then perhaps Pilate hoped to be able to dismiss the charges on the basis of public reaction. Because of his distasteful relationship with Jewish leaders, he would be pleased to see a public demonstration against them and their decisions. So Pilate reaffirmed his opinion of Jesus' innocence, reinforced by Herod's indifference to the legal charges. He would punish him by scourging (see the commentary on 18:33 about *flogging*), but then set Jesus free.

Pilate may have expected to receive public support for this decision. However, the crowd present called for the release of another prisoner, Barabbas (called Jesus Barabbas in some manuscripts), and then later for Jesus to be crucified (verse 21). This public response may have been because the larger group was actually the Sanhedrin members, or the crowd had been recruited and organized to support the charges against Jesus. Luke is generous in his portrayal of Pilate's attitude toward Jesus, as he is toward Romans in general. In spite of the crowd's request for the release of Barabbas instead of Jesus, Pilate sought to change their attitude (verse 20). Then he reaffirmed his previous opinion and decision, even as the crowd shouted for Jesus to be crucified.

According to Luke, the urgent and demanding voices of the crowd *prevailed.* John's account adds another factor which could explain the change in Pilate's stand. Some of the accusers said to Pilate, *If you release this man, you are not Caesar's friend; every one who makes himself a king sets himself against Caesar* (John 19:12). This would have been a type of pressure to which Pilate would have been susceptible. In any event, Pilate had found the expressed sentiment building more against him than against the Jewish leaders.

Since Passover marked the celebration of deliverance from bondage and the liberation of the Jewish people, it may well have been a custom for one Jewish prisoner to be released as a part of the symbolic ceremonies of recollection. Thus Barabbas, leader of a violent rebellion, was released while Jesus was *delivered up to their will* (verse 25).

Procession to Calvary (23:26-32)

Missing from Luke's account is the scourging by the Roman soldiers and the painful mockery of the crown of thorns reported in other Gospel accounts (Matthew 27:27-30; Mark 15:16-19).

Cyrene (verse 26) was an important capital city on the north coast of Africa, founded by Greeks. The man named Simon from this city may have been a Jew coming to Jerusalem for the Passover. Mark identifies him as the father of Alexander and Rufus, persons known to the early Christians (Mark 15:21; Romans 16:13).

Part of the punishment of crucifixion usually was the carrying of one's own cross to the site of execution. Tradition reports that Jesus carried the cross part of the way. Weakened by scourging and loss of sleep, Jesus either collapsed beneath its weight or moved too slowly. The execution had to be completed before the sabbath, which began at sunset. Thus Simon of Cyrene was pressed into service to carry the cross.

When the procession moved from Pilate's palace down the roadway toward Golgotha, that portion of the populace devoted to Jesus but excluded from Pilate's courtyard now joined the procession. The type of public indignation that the Jewish leaders had feared now manifested itself in the form of profound grief and despair (verse 27), especially among women, who had sensed in Jesus a heightened respect for their personhood and a sensitivity to their need. The counsel of Jesus to these women (verses 28-31) to feel sorry for themselves rather than for him included a repetition of warnings spoken as he had approached Jerusalem six days earlier (19:41-44) and during this last week (21:23-24). Verse 30 is a quotation from Hosea 10:8b. Verse 31 is a form of an old proverb, suggesting that if this destruction can come to a good man, what more extreme destruction will yet come upon the evil?

Crucifixion was the Roman form of execution for criminals, and multiple executions were a convenience to those charged with arranging and supervising executions.

Crucifixion (23:33-49)

The place of crucifixion was a skull-shaped hill. The Aramaic name was *Golgotha.* Luke uses its translated meaning, *the skull* (verse 33). Golgotha was rendered into Greek with the word *kranion,* which was then rendered into Latin as *calvaria,* from which we have obtained the English word *Calvary.* Calvary is the Latin form and Golgotha the Aramaic form of the name of the skull-shaped hill, appropriate for executions.

The method of crucifixion involved attaching a person's arms by ropes or nails to a cross-beam affixed to an upright wooden beam. Sometimes there was support to the legs by placing a raised projection on the upright beam, upon which they could be placed. A painful death came through exposure and bodily stress rather than by blood loss, sometimes over a long period of days rather than hours.

The first petition from the cross, *Father, forgive them . . .* (verse 34) appears only in Luke's account. It does not appear in all the ancient manuscripts of Luke, but it is authentic to the nature of Jesus and reflects the intimate at-homeness in the relationship between Jesus and God.

Any clothing or possessions still in the hands of those executed could be taken by the soldiers carrying out the crucifixion. So they gambled (*cast lots*) for his remaining clothing (verse 34), which they had stripped from him before placing him on the cross. An experience like this had been spoken of in Psalm 22:18.

The people watched, perhaps with hurt and dismay. But the taunt of the rulers (verse 35) was to the effect that if Jesus was the Messiah and God's chosen one, which his followers had claimed, then he could demonstrate it now by powerfully stepping off the cross. This was a temptation similar in nature to that third temptation in the wilderness (4:9-12)—use a miraculous shortcut to win recognition and allegiance.

The *vinegar* (NIV; NRSV = *sour wine*) offered by the soldiers may have been wine with a drug to ease the pain, often offered in pity to those being executed. However, it is also possible that it was only vinegar offered as though it were a sedative, as part of their mockery of this so-called *king of the Jews.* Over the cross an inscription was usually placed stating the nature of the crime as a warning to onlookers. Over Jesus' cross the inscription was, *This is the King of the Jews* (verse 38). John's account reports Pilate as the instigator of the inscription, and later his defense of it when challenged (see John 19:19-22).

One of the criminals picked up the taunt of the *rulers* and turned it into a petition to Jesus, as Christ, to save them all. Surprisingly, the other criminal confessed that he belonged where he was, in contrast to Jesus' innocence (verse 41). The criminal's prayer is simple but beautiful. When he knew not what to seek and knew that he did not merit seeking any favor, he simply petitioned. *Remember me . . .* (verse 42), in the confidence that Jesus would know what he needed and provide more than he deserved. Somehow, he had come to faith in Jesus' kingly power. Jesus' promise that they would be together that day *in Paradise* presents a different concept of what awaits after death from the traditional Jewish concept of

Sheol (see commentary on 12:5). This concept would become more prevalent in Jewish thinking about life beyond death and would occupy a central place in Christian expectations.

The sixth hour (NIV; NRSV = *noon*) would be midday and *the ninth hour* would be 3:00 P.M. Either an eclipse of the sun took place or dark clouds covered the sun to match the dark deeds of these hours.

In the Temple there was an ornate curtain or veil which separated the Holy of Holies, where the ark of the covenant was located, from the Holy Place (see Exodus 26:31-35 for a detailed description of this veil). This curtain was lifted only once a year when the high priest could alone enter the Holy of Holies to pray for forgiveness for the people. At Jesus' death the curtain was torn apart (verse 45), signifying that now there was direct access into God's holy presence for all, through Christ's sacrifice.

The final cry of Jesus from the cross in Luke's account is a quotation by Jesus of Psalm 31:5. This signifies his continued attitude of respect and participation for the scriptural tradition of his ancestry as well as his identification with the feelings of that psalmist. It is Jesus' ultimate expression of commitment to God.

Roman soldiers had taken over from the Jewish guard the custody of Jesus from the time of his arrival before Pilate through the implementation of the crucifixion. A centurion originally supervised one hundred soldiers. Thus the centurion who affirms Jesus' innocence may have been in charge of those soldiers carrying out the execution. Once again Luke presents a Roman in a good light.

The dismayed and sorrowful crowd went home *beating their breasts* (verse 48). This was a symbolic and traditional way of expressing grief. The women mentioned were the same ones whom Jesus had addressed on his way to the hill of the skull.

142

§ § § § § § §

The Message of Luke 22:55–23:49

The death of a prominent person always has a strange fascination for us. Every detail becomes important. Yet of all such deaths none has equaled the attention given to the death of Jesus. The reason lies beyond the method of his dying, as unique as that was. For Luke, and many others, the reason for the fascination with this man's death was that God was in this picture in a unique way. This death was not just that of an itinerant prophet named Jesus, but one who was seen as the Christ of God.

Luke's account of the crucifixion tells us of a God who moves into the midst of life's struggles and needs and into the depth of life's sorrows and injustices. In so doing, the divine style is that of reconciling love expressed through servanthood. Luke wants us to see the cross as a marker erected on this earth of ours to tell us of a God whose concern was for this world and all within it, and who travails with us for it.

At this point Luke would probably also want us to recall the words of Jesus he recorded in 14:27: *Whoever does not bear his own cross and come after me, cannot be my disciple.* The cross requires us to leave our customary ways and hold onto it. We grasp it not just for the comfort and compassion it offers, and we take up the challenge it presents to us. If we adhere to its demands, the cross will change our lives.

§ § § § § § §

LUKE 23:50–24:53

Introduction to These Chapters

This section begins with solemn removal from the
cross and burial of the body of Jesus. Simultaneously, the
hopes and spirits of the followers of Jesus had sunk to
the ground with that burial.

But *on the first day of the week* joy came in the morning.
The resurrection of Jesus broke down despair and raised
up new hopes through the encounters that followed. The
result is that the narrative ends finding the disciples *with
great joy* and *blessing God.* The events of this section are as
follows:

I. Burial and Final Tributes (23:50–24:1)
II. The Exciting Discovery (24:2-11)
III. Appearance on the Road (24:12-35)
IV. Appearance to the Disciples (24:36-43)
V. A Commission Given (24:44-49)
VI. Blessing and Response (24:50-53)

Burial and Final Tributes (23:50–24:1)

The location of Arimathea is not known. Since Luke
identifies it as a Jewish town, Joseph would have been a
prominent resident of that community, since he was a
member of the *council,* or Sanhedrin. In describing him as
a *righteous man,* Luke would mean that he was obedient
to the Mosaic law through which righteousness was
obtained. In spite of this loyalty, he had not felt Jesus
was guilty of a disobedience deserving death (verse 51).

To be a *good* man would mean he was sincere in his faith in God and in relationships with others. Since the kingdom of God was a primary focus in Jesus' preaching, followers of Jesus were often identified as "looking for the kingdom of God." However, in John's account Joseph is described as a secret disciple of Jesus *for fear of the Jews* (John 19:38).

Unless the body of an executed criminal was claimed, it would be left to scavengers. Joseph prevented that happening to the body of Jesus. However, he had to move rapidly, for the sabbath was near at hand. The burial had to take place before the sabbath began. The rock-hewn tomb may have been cut into a rocky cliff or hillside, thus resembling a cave. Across the entrance opening would be placed a large circular stone which could be rolled aside to open the entrance.

The women who had come with Jesus from Galilee were the same ones who had been present earlier in the week and who had followed Jesus as he was taken to Golgotha. They only had time to inspect the tomb and return to their lodging before the sabbath began. There they began to prepare *spices and ointments* (NRSV; NIV = *perfumes*) which would be placed upon the body. This was the ancient substitute for embalming. These ointments would provide some preservative for the body and the spices would overcome the odors from the body's decaying.

The sabbath extended from Friday at sundown to Saturday at sundown and was counted as the seventh day of the week. Therefore, the *first day of the week* at dawn would be the equivalent of Sunday morning. The Christian church would change its day of worship from the Jewish sabbath time to Sunday to celebrate the resurrection of Christ. Each Sunday's gathering would be a renewed celebration of the Resurrection.

The Exciting Discovery (24:2-11)

The women who came to carry out the embalming were shocked first by finding no body and then by finding *two men* in dazzling apparel (verse 4). These were angelic beings. These messengers not only confirmed that Jesus had been raised, but recalled for them what Jesus had predicted about himself even before the journey to Jerusalem had begun (9:22). Mary Magdalene, or Mary of Magdala, and Joanna were first identified by Luke in 8:2 in Galilee as persons who had been healed and who provided for the disciples from their resources. The other Mary listed was the mother of one of the disciples, James, son of Alphaeus (6:15). The women's report seemed to be a fabrication born out of emotion, and was not believed.

Appearance on the Road (24:12-35)

The site of Emmaus (verse 13) is uncertain. The name meant *warm springs*. This is the only mention of Emmaus in the Bible. Although Mark makes mention of an appearance of Jesus to two persons traveling through the countryside (Mark 16:12-13), only Luke gives the account in some detail.

Two of them (verse 13) would mean two of the eleven apostles and the *rest* to whom the women had reported after visiting the tomb. Whether they were men or women is not stated.

No reason is given as to why they *were kept from recognizing* Jesus (verse 16). The implication is that this was by divine action. Or it may simply be that they did not recognize Jesus in his resurrected form, especially since they did not believe what the women had reported.

Cleopas is not clearly identified. It may have been a shortened from of the Greek word *Cleopatros*, from which the name Cleopatra comes. Tradition has designated the other companion as being named Simon, in the light of the reference in verse 34.

The conversation recorded in verses 19-25 summarizes some of the convictions of the early followers about Jesus, such as *a prophet mighty in deed and word before God* (verse 19), and *he was the one to redeem Israel* (verse 21). Also they confirm that the women had made a report about an empty tomb and a vision of angels. They indicate that some *went to the tomb* to see for themselves (verse 24). Some of the early manuscripts of Luke do have an additional verse, which reports: *Peter rose and ran to the tomb; stooping and looking in, he saw the linen cloths by themselves; and he went home wondering at what had happened.*

Foolish (verse 25) is from a Greek word meaning *not understanding. Slow of heart* means slow to believe with one's heart. Jesus in this conversation clearly identified himself as the fulfillment of the messianic hope rooted in the ancient promises to the patriarchs and preached by the prophets.

Their invitation to Jesus to stay with them was an expression not only of hospitality but also of an affinity they felt with him and a desire to learn more from him. Jesus was *recognized* as he blessed and broke the bread (verse 30). Luke states, *their eyes were opened* . . . (verse 31). This could mean that in the act of blessing and breaking bread, they recalled Jesus doing the same many times and maybe were present at the Last Supper, when Jesus blessed and shared the bread. The way he did it may have brought to their awareness who he was. Also, as he broke bread, they may have noted the nail prints in his hands. Later they would tell the other disciples *how he was known* to them *in the breaking of the bread* (verse 35).

It was now nighttime. The fact that they returned to Jerusalem *that same hour* (verse 33, NRSV; NIV = at once) rather than waiting until daybreak shows their excitement over this discovery. The phrase *our hearts burning within us,* used to describe their excitement, may be a use of the similar imagery in Psalm 39:3 or Jeremiah 20:9.

Appearance to the Disciples (24:36-43)

Some ancient manuscripts state that Jesus' first word at this unexpected reunion with his disciples was the traditional Jewish greeting, "Shalom" ("Peace be with you").

The word *ghost* (verse 37) is the Greek word for *spirit*. The invitation to touch him, especially his hands and feet where the nail or rope marks would be, was to prove that he had a physical form, not just a spirit form. John adds drama to this episode by describing how the doubting Thomas, who refused to believe in the resurrection unless he could touch Jesus' wounds in his hand and side, was invited by Jesus to do so (John 20:24-29). Eating *a piece of broiled fish* added to the evidence of his physical reality (verses 42-43).

A Commission Given (24:44-49)

As Luke records Jesus' words to the disciples, the emphasis of Jesus was still on affirming that he was the fulfillment of the Judaic scriptural tradition (verse 44) regarding the Messiah and Son of man. It was important to Luke in connection with his purposes for writing this Gospel account that this fulfillment by Jesus be obvious and emphasized for the Jewish readers. Jesus again used the method of recalling to his disciples what he had said about himself on several occasions but which then they did not fully understand (see 18:31-33; 22:37). He used scriptural passages that could describe or make understandable what had happened to him and through him: . . . *repentance and forgiveness of sins is to be preached in his name to all nations* . . . (verse 47).

The starting place for this witness was to be Jerusalem. The commission given to them by Jesus was that they were to be the beginning *witnesses* (verse 48). The witness to the world was to begin with their witness where they now were. Remember that *witness* is a translation of the Greek word *martyr*. Some of this witnessing to the world would require, and be through, martyrdom.

With the commission was a promise by Jesus to *send what* God has *promised* (verse 49). John's account identifies this promise as the Holy Spirit (John 14:26; 20:22), as predicted by the prophet Joel (Joel 2:28-29). The demanding and crucial task of witnessing would be undergirded and empowered by the gift, presence, and power of the Holy Spirit. As previously stated, Jesus testified that God never calls us to a task greater than the resources God makes available to enable its achievement. They would be *clothed with power from on high* before they left Jerusalem, where they were to wait.

Blessing and Response (24:50-53)

Jesus and his disciples had passed through Bethany in the suburbs of Jerusalem as they came to the city from Jericho for this last week. Now, after all that had transpired in that week, Jesus led his disciples back to Bethany on their way out. He was different and they were different, and nothing would ever be the same again.

In Acts 1:6-12 Luke describes in more detail the conversation of Jesus with his disciples in this setting. With the blessing of Jesus came again the promise of power and enablement through the Holy Spirit. The blessing would take the form of the Spirit. To state it otherwise, Jesus' real blessing was the blessing of his continuance in their midst through the Holy Spirit, even though he would leave them physically (verse 51).

The disciples returned to Jerusalem from this site, which must have been near or on the Mount of Olives (Acts 1:12). They came *with great joy* (verse 52) because of the awareness of Christ being risen and the promise of power to come. They went to the *upper room, where they were staying* and where they *with one accord devoted themselves to prayer* (Acts 1:13-14).

Luke ends this first work by reporting that out of joy and thanksgiving they returned to the Temple where they had spent so much of their time learning and struggling through the last week with Jesus. They came now not to mourn, but to give thanks and wait with hope.

§ § § § § § §

The Message of Luke 23:50–24:53

It was a shattering experience for these women to face an open tomb wherein the body of Jesus no longer lay. If they had not been able to do anything for Jesus during his suffering, at least they could do something for his body in death. But they sought Jesus where he was not to be found, for the miracle had happened. For those of us who have lowered our vision of possibilities to only the expected, the unexpected is a miracle. Yet God brings that miracle to us, as to the women, often enough to make us aware that the unpredictable is a part of life's experiences. This awareness can be our sustenance and hope.

Furthermore, Luke shows us that Christ was to be found in new places. Christ outdistanced any attempt to imprison him in a tomb. He goes before us. As we go out beyond our present lifestyles, our pre-conditioned expectations of Jesus or any structure that would confine him, there we will find Christ. Luke calls us to a relationship with Christ that is ever moving and not simply waiting, exploring and not simply affirming what we already know.

The last paragraphs of Luke's account point outward. Jesus said, *Repentance and forgiveness of sins is to be preached in his name in all nations, beginning from Jerusalem.* Then Christ walked with them out of their narrow world toward the wider world. Through his Spirit Christ continues to lead, walking with us and in us. We are the channel through which his risen presence moves into the world.

To summarize, Luke blesses us in his *orderly account* by unveiling for us a Christ who at personal risk came in love, informed by his words, healed by his touch, hurt with us and then for us. And still, centuries after his death, he remains with us, calling us and enabling us by his risen presence and spirit to do the same for others.

§ § § § § § §

Glossary of Terms

Annas: The high priest from A.D. 6/7 to about 15.

Arimathea: A Jewish town whose present site is uncertain. There Joseph, who arranged for the burial of Jesus, was a prominent resident.

Augustus: The title given by the Roman Senate in 27 B.C. to Gaius Julius Caesar Octavianus, who then was ruler of the Roman Empire, at the time of the birth of Jesus.

Barabbas: A prisoner at the time of Jesus' arrest who was a leader of an insurrection resulting in deaths.

Beelzebul: A name or title for the prince of devils who had power over evil. The word may have arisen from the pagan god, Baal, or a god of Ekron with a similar name.

Bethany: A town on the Mount of Olives east of Jerusalem. The name means *house of the poor* or *afflicted*.

Bethlehem: A small town six miles southwest of Jerusalem that was the ancestral home of David (1 Samuel 17:15) and the location of the story of Ruth (Ruth 1:1-2). The name is usually interpreted to mean *house of bread*.

Bethphage: A village east of Bethany or near the road from Jericho to Jerusalem. The name means *house of unripe figs*.

Bethsaida: A town near Lake Gennesaret near the Jordan River with a name meaning *house of the fisher*.

Caiaphas: Appointed high priest by Valerius Gratus in A.D. 18, serving until removed from office in A.D. 36 or 37.

Capernaum: An important town on the northwest coast of the Sea of Galilee with a name meaning *village of Nahum*.

Chorazin: A city of Galilee on the hills near Capernaum where Jesus preached but residents were unresponsive.

Cleopas: One of two followers whom the risen Christ accompanied on a journey to Emmaus. The name may be a shortened form of the Greek word, *Cleopatros,* from which the name *Cleopatra* comes. Cleopas may have been the father of James.

Cyrene: An important capital city on the north coast of Africa, founded by Greeks; home of Lucius who became a leader in the church at Antioch (Acts 13:1).

Elizabeth, Elisabeth: Wife of the priest Zechariah, and mother of John the Baptist. Her name meant *God is an oath.*

Emmaus: A town seven miles from Jerusalem. The name meant *warm springs,* but the site is uncertain.

Gabriel: An angel or messenger of God, later regarded as an archangel, whose activities are described in 1 and 2 Enoch. He is introduced in the Bible as an interpreter in Daniel 8:16-17.

Galilee: A word that means *circle* or *region,* the name of an area in northern Palestine on the western side of the Sea of Galilee and its tributaries. Nazareth and Capernaum were located in Galilee.

Gennesaret, Sea of: Sometimes used interchangeably for the Sea of Galilee, but technically it is that portion of the sea adjacent to a fertile valley on the northwest shore called Gennesaret.

Gerasenes: Persons from Gerasa, a site on the east shore of the Sea of Galilee. Also called Gadarenes in some translations with the site called Gadara.

Hades: The abode of the dead, *Sheol* in the Old Testament.

Herod: The name of a dynasty that ruled Jewish Palestine under Roman authority from 37 B.C. to A.D. 70. Herod the Great was ruler at the time of Jesus' birth. A son, Herod Antipas, was ruler at the time of the crucifixion.

Herodias: Was first married to her father's half-brother, Philip. From this union Salome was born. Later she was married to Herod Antipas while Philip was still alive.

James: A fisherman on the Sea of Galilee who became one of the twelve disciples of Jesus. Brother of John, another disciple, and son of Zebedee. Died as a martyr under Herod

Agrippa I (Acts 12:1-2). Another person named James was also one of the Twelve. Son of Alphaeus, his name is included in the lists of disciples, but in no other reference in the Gospels or Acts.

John: Brother of James and son of Zebedee, and a fisherman with them, as well as one of the Twelve. Tradition locates him as becoming a leader in the church at Ephesus. The name means *God has been gracious*.

Joseph: (1) The husband of Mary, mother of Jesus. His vocation as a carpenter is inferred by the reference in Mark to Jesus being a carpenter (Mark 6:3). He is only mentioned in the Gospels in connection with the stories of Jesus' childhood.

(2) Known as *Joseph of Arimathea* (see above). He was a member of the Sanhedrin, the ruling council of the Jewish religion. He took responsibility for the body of Jesus after Jesus' death and placed it in his own tomb.

Judas: (1) The son or brother of James, who became one of the twelve disciples. He is also called Thaddaeus. The name *Judas* was a form of *Judah*. He is a different person from Judas Iscariot.

(2) Son of Simon Iscariot with a name subject to various translations. *Iscariot* probably meant *from Kerioth*, a place of uncertain location. Betrayer of Jesus, Judas was one of the twelve disciples.

Judea: A region in southern Palestine west of the northern part of the Dead Sea. Before the Exile it was called Judah. Here Bethlehem was located.

Legion: The largest subdivision of the Roman army, consisting of 4,500 to 6,000 men. The mentally ill man chose this name to symbolize his feeling of the immensity of the evil influences within him.

Leprosy: From a Hebrew word meaning *scourge*, it referred to an eruptive skin disease which began as a scab and spread, turning the hair white in the affected area and resulting in raw flesh. The victim was considered unclean and was excluded from the community.

Levi: Two different ancestors of Jesus mentioned in the geneology. Also a tax collector in Capernaum who became a follower of Jesus. Matthew's account gives this person the name of *Matthew* (9:9). However, Luke makes no attempt to relate the two. Levi is described here as a follower and Matthew is listed among the twelve chosen apostles (6:15).

Lysanias: A subject prince, or tetrarch, of an area northwest of Damascus, about whom little is known.

Martha: Sister of Mary and Lazarus of Bethany. The name means *lady* or *mistress*.

Mary: The name is a form of the Hebrew word *Miriam*. At least four persons with that name appear in Luke's account:

(1) A peasant woman, possibly of Levitic descent, who became the mother of Jesus.

(2) Known as Mary Magdalene, she was from Magdala on the southwest coast of the Sea of Galilee, and was a follower of Jesus in whom some type of evil influence or illness had been taken away by Jesus.

(3) A sister of Martha and Lazarus who lived with them in Bethany or a place in southern Galilee. In the fourth Gospel (John 12:3) she is identified as the one who anoints Jesus with oil (see Luke 7:37-38).

(4) The mother of James the apostle, identified in John 19:25 as the wife of Clopas. She was at the crucifixion and visited the empty tomb.

Nain: A village five miles southeast of Nazareth and twenty-five miles from Capernaum. The name means *pleasant* because from it there is a lovely view of the Plain of Esdraelon.

Nazareth: The village in Galilee where Jesus was raised, located fifteen miles southwest of the Sea of Galilee at an altitude of 1,300 feet.

Nineveh: The capital of Assyria to which the prophet Jonah preached, resulting in widespread repentance (Jonah 3).

Olivet (Mount of Olives): A ridge of hills east of Jerusalem about a mile from north to south and 200 feet above the site of the Temple. Mentioned in the Old Testament in 2 Samuel 15:30 and Zechariah 14:4.

Passover: Jewish festival celebrating the sparing of the Hebrew first-born immediately prior to the Exodus. Combines with the feast of Unleavened Bread.

Phanual: Father of Anna the prophetess and a member of the tribe of Asher.

Pharisees: The name is from an Aramaic word meaning *separated*. They were one of the chief Jewish parties or sects with a central focus on rigid obedience to the law, continuation of ritual traditions, and religious purity with its resulting separation in lifestyle and relationships. Although their perspective arose during the Exile and became structured after the Exile, they are first mentioned by the historian Josephus during the reign of John Hyrcanus (135-105 B.C.).

Philip: (1) A son of Herod the Great and Cleopatra of Jerusalem, he was tetrarch of an area between the Sea of Galilee and Damascus.

(2) One of the Twelve, he was from Bethsaida. More references to him appear in John (1:43-48; 6:5, 7; 12:20-23). He is not the same person as Philip the evangelist (Acts 21:8).

Pontius Pilate: The Roman procurator in Judea, A.D. 26-36, who was the judge at the trial of Jesus. He was immensely disliked by the Jews because he had permitted his troops to carry ensigns with images of the emperor on them into Jerusalem and had taken sacred money to use for building a water channel. After an attack upon some Samaritans, Pilate was ordered to Rome to answer to the emperor. One undocumented report has him assigned to southern France, where he ultimately committed suicide.

Quirinius: The Roman governor of Syria appointed in A.D. 6, who took a census reported by Josephus. However, the date of this census does not appear to agree with the one described by Luke, because Herod, mentioned by Luke as the ruler at the time of Jesus' birth, died in 4 B.C.

Sabbath: This Hebrew word means *rest* or *cessation*. In Jewish law it was decreed as a day of rest to be observed (Exodus 20:8-11) every seven days in recollection of God's resting after Creation (Genesis 2:1-3).

Sadducees: A Jewish party or sect deriving their name from Zadok the priest (about 300 B.C.). They took as authority only the law itself and not inherited commentaries on the law, and allowed for private interpretation. Members appear to have been primarily from the priestly aristocracy.

Samaria: The name of a city and a district. The city was the capital of Israel, built when Omri was the king, and located forty-two miles north of Jerusalem. The district was in central Palestine between Galilee and Judea.

Sidon: A city of the Canaanites on the seacoast twenty-two miles north of Tyre.

Simeon: A devout Jew who was looking for the Messiah and about whom nothing more is known beyond Luke's description.

Simon: (1) A member of the Zealots, a group of opponents to Roman rule, who became one of the Twelve.

(2) Host for a dinner where a woman came in unexpectedly and anointed Jesus with oil. He was a Pharisee.

(3) A resident of Cyrene (see above) in North Africa. Probably a Jew who came to Jerusalem for the Passover.

Susanna: The name comes from a Hebrew word meaning *lily*. She was one of the women who ministered to Jesus.

Tetrarch: A ruler of less prominence and territory than a king, usually responsible for a district.

Theophilus: The name means *friend of God*. To this person (or type of person) the books of Luke and Acts are addressed.

Tiberius: His full name and title was Tiberius Claudius Caesar Augustus, the Roman emperor ruling from A.D. 14-37.

Tyre: A central city of Phoenicia on the Mediterranean Sea.

Zacchaeus: A tax collector of Jericho with administrative responsibility for other collectors.

Zarephath: With a name meaning *to dye*, this was a Phoenician town on the Mediterranean coast near Sidon where dye was produced.

Zebedee: Husband of Salome and father of James and John, he was also a fisherman.

Zechariah: A priest who was father of John the Baptist.

Guide to Pronunciation

Arimathea: Air-ah-mah-THEE-ah
Augustus: Ah-GUS-tus
Barabbas: Bah-RAB-us
Beelzebul: Bee-EHL-ze-bul
Bethany: BETH-ah-nee
Bethphage: BETH-fay-je
Bethsaida: Beth-SAY-eh-dah
Caiaphas: KIGH-ah-fus
Capernaum: Kah-PURR-nay-um
Chorazim: KORE-ah-zim
Cleopas: KLEE-oh-pus
Cyrene: Sigh-REE-nee
Gennesaret: Geh-NESS-eh-ret
Gerasenes: GAIR-ah-zenes
Nain: NANE or NAY-een
Phanuel: FAN-you-ehl
Quirinius: Kwih-RIHN-ee-us
Sadducees: SAD-you-seez
Tiberius: Tie-BEER-ee-us
Trachonitus: Trak-uh-NIGHT-us
Zacchaeus: Zak-EE-us
Zarephath: ZARE-eh-FATH
Zebedee: ZEH-beh-dee
Zechariah: Zek-eh-RIGH-ah

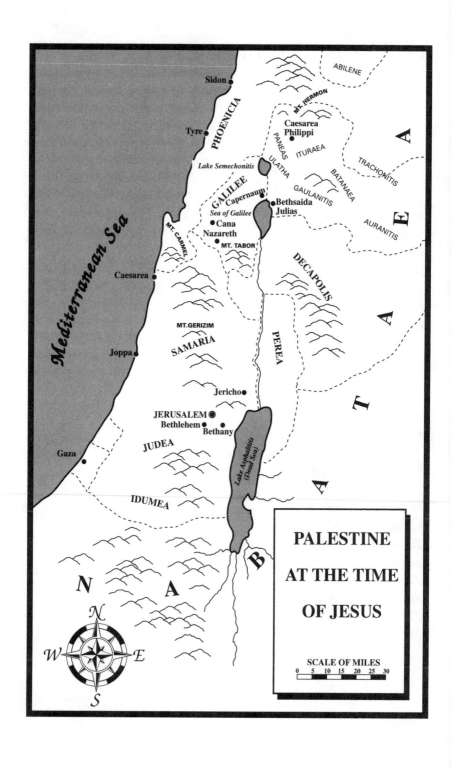

PALESTINE

AT THE TIME

OF JESUS

SCALE OF MILES

0   5   10   15   20   25   30